PAiLS

*20 Years from Now,
What Will You Wish
You Had Done Today?*

New York Times Bestselling Author
CHRIS BRADY

FOREWORD BY *NEW YORK TIMES* BESTSELLING AUTHOR
ORRIN WOODWARD

Copyright © 2014 by Chris Brady
All rights reserved. No part of this book may be reproduced or transmitted in any form or by any means, electronic or mechanical, including photocopying and recording, or by any information storage and retrieval system, without the written permission of Obstaclés Press. Inquiries should be sent to the publisher.

Obstaclés Press and the Obstaclés logo are trademarks of Life.

First Edition, February 2014

Published by:
Obstaclés Press
200 Commonwealth Court
Cary, NC 27511

chrisbrady.com

ISBN: 979-8-218-44604-8

Scripture quotations are taken from the NEW AMERICAN STANDARD BIBLE®, Copyright © 1960, 1962, 1963, 1968, 1971, 1972, 1973, 1975, 1977, 1995 by The Lockman Foundation. Used by permission.

Book design by Norm Williams, nwa-inc.com

Printed in the United States of America

To be what is called happy, one should have (1) something to live on, (2) something to live for, and (3) something to die for. The lack of one of these is drama. The lack of two results in tragedy.

—Cyprian Norwid, Nineteenth-Century Polish Poet

CONTENTS

Foreword — 7

Introduction — 9

Potential: What Will You Do?

1. Monument — 19
2. Place — 31

Actualization: How Will You Do It?

3. Difficulty — 47
4. Exertion — 57
5. Immersion — 69
6. Some — 81

Legacy (and Spillage): What Will It Matter?

7. Meaning — 93
8. Originality — 105
9. Spillage — 115
10. Masterpiece — 127

Epilogue — 137

Acknowledgments — 139

FOREWORD

When *New York Times* bestselling author and speaker Chris Brady notified me that he was sending a hard copy of his latest book to me, I was intrigued. For any time I read his works, I find my mind expanded, my heart encouraged, and my resolve strengthened. Although I have partnered with Chris for nearly twenty years, I still find myself marveling at his ability to communicate truth in a disarming fashion. Further, he somehow does this while making everyone laugh hysterically. Seriously, the only thing more fun than reading a Chris Brady book is having the privilege of sitting in the front row when he is speaking.

In any event, when I received the book, I devoured it in a matter of hours. Thankfully, no one was home, since there were several times when Chris brought me to tears—sometimes with his humor and other times with his poignancy. Anyone who has read Chris's critically acclaimed book *A Month of Italy* can relate to what I am saying. Nonetheless, this book breaks new ground for the author as it addresses an important issue for today's youth (and people of all ages, for that matter), namely, what is the best way to pursue one's life goals and dreams?

In answering that question, Chris develops a framework for life and happiness that is both innovative and compelling. In fact, Chris's four-layer ziggurat has become the basis for mentoring my own teenagers as they prepare for their journeys through life. Starting with Preparatory Experiences and a Pragmatic Occupation, Chris explains how these two layers can be the foundation for chasing one's Passionate Pursuit, culminating in fulfilling one's Purposeful Calling. They say genius is the ability to make the complex seem simple. Accordingly, the first chapter alone qualifies Chris for Mensa membership as he has simplified one's life into four layers that build upon one another. Such insight is priceless.

Taking this information, I quickly reviewed in my mind the many people I have modeled, mentored, and studied to confirm the truthfulness of the life ziggurat. Every successful person utilizes the principles in this book, whether they realize it or not. Fortunately, with the writing of this book, Chris has provided the next generation with a revolutionary approach to living that breaks down the half-truths and outright fallacies that hold people back from achieving their purpose in life.

Finally, when taking any advice in life, it is important to identify whether the person has "fruit on the tree" in the area he proposes to teach. Having known Chris since both of us were eighteen-year-old college kids, I have been blessed to watch him build his life ziggurat. From his preparatory experiences in motocross racing to his pragmatic career as an engineer, Chris laid the foundation necessary to pursue his passion. Indeed, in the time after his eight- to ten-hour workdays, he progressively developed mastery in the fields of writing, speaking, and leading.

After five years of toiling in anonymity, Chris broke into the mainstream with a string of bestselling books (having sold over a million copies in seven languages) and speaking engagements around the world in front of tens of thousands of people. Moreover, he has supported numerous charitable works through his board position in All Grace Outreach Ministries. In addition, Chris and his lovely wife Terri are nurturing parents to four entrepreneurially minded children. To wrap up, I believe the best teachers model before they message, and Chris Brady's life has authentically modeled the message he illuminates here.

Orrin Woodward
New York Times Bestselling Author
Founder of Life

INTRODUCTION

In an age and place where people are not forced into a particular occupation or consumed on a daily basis with the very act of survival, they are instead left with choices about what they will do with their lives. Gandalf the wizard perhaps most succinctly stated this in the movie *The Lord of the Rings: The Fellowship of the Ring*: "All we have to decide is what to do with the time that is given to us."

For many of us, however, this is easier said than done. Instead of deciding, we go through a dance of not deciding, until circumstances and events decide for us. In the end, we're merely *at the end*, neither having followed a definite plan nor even having considered what we were about along the way.

Bronnie Ware, a woman who worked for years with the dying, wrote an article sharing "The Top Five Regrets of the Dying":

1. I wish I'd had the courage to live a life true to myself, not the life others expected of me.
2. I wish I hadn't worked so hard.
3. I wish I'd had the courage to express my feelings.
4. I wish I had stayed in touch with my friends.
5. I wish I had let myself be happier.

There are many such studies. What is striking is how similar the results all seem to be. It appears that when it comes to the living of our lives, we are all a bunch of amateurs. We tend to miss the main things a large part of the time.

Frederic Tudor had a bent toward business from an early age. Deciding to skip the Harvard education that was expected of him as the son of a wealthy lawyer, Tudor instead got the idea to ship ice from his family's New England farm to Cuba and the Caribbean. He would have his employees carve out lake ice in rectangular blocks that could be stacked closely together in a ship's hull. Then they would cover the stack with straw and wood chips for insulation from the heat. Upon arrival in the hotter climates, the slightly depleted ice would be moved into icehouses and sold to the wealthy in small quantities as a luxury for their drinks. Over those next early decades of the 1800s, however, ice became more and more useful in food storage, and the Tudor ice business grew exponentially.

At some point in the development of his thriving business, Tudor hauled apples packed around his ice to the south and brought bananas, limes, oranges, and pears around remaining ice blocks on return journeys back to the north. Although these first efforts at transporting tropical fruit failed miserably, he had inadvertently invented refrigerated transport! For some reason, however, Tudor never concentrated on this staggering discovery and distracted himself instead with speculating in coffee futures. As a result, his main business of ice hauling languished. In the end, Tudor recovered his losses in coffee futures by focusing again on hauling ice, leaving the enormous discovery of refrigerated transport to be developed by others years later. Evidently, Tudor missed the invention of refrigerated freight because he considered himself to be in the ice shipping business.

Many people use up the days of their lives and waste the time they've been given because they, much like Tudor, have the wrong idea of what it is they are doing. Life is not about advancing day by day through the calendar, merely finding something that works financially and trying to enjoy a little time off on the weekends. It is not about "getting by" or "doing pretty well." There is much more at stake than any of that. It is also not about heading for happiness directly, the endless pursuit of pleasure,

INTRODUCTION

or achieving fame and financial success. As we will see, those who live in such a way are missing the bigger picture of who they could be and are merely hauling ice instead.

Viktor Frankl was a psychiatrist in Germany during World War II. He turned down his chance to leave the country on an exit visa because he felt duty-bound to stay behind and be with his aging parents as the Nazi threat loomed larger. Eventually, he and his entire family were hauled off to concentration camps. His parents, brother, and pregnant wife were all killed. Frankl himself survived the horror of four different camps over the course of three years, emerging with a firsthand case study of human psychiatry that would be the basis of his work for the rest of his life.

Frankl wrote, "Man's search for meaning is the primary motivation in his life.... This meaning is unique and specific in that it must and can be fulfilled by him alone." Frankl further wrote, "Everyone has his own specific vocation or mission in life to carry out a concrete assignment which demands fulfillment. Therein he cannot be replaced, nor can his life be repeated. Thus, everyone's task is as unique as is his specific opportunity to implement it."

It seems that if Frankl was correct, part of the consideration of what to do with our time must concentrate upon *meaning*. And in the pursuit of that meaning, Frankl suggested that there is a specific mission in life unique to each of us. So far, so good. But still, one question underlies all of this. And that question is: *How?* How does one go about choosing what to do with the days that are left for him or her? How does one find and pursue a meaningful life? And just how, exactly, does one go about uncovering his or her unique mission in life?

For thousands of years, humans have used maps to navigate unknown territory (presumably because they didn't have Gandalf nearby). The task of seeking to answer these questions about pursuing a life of meaning strikes me as much like navigating dangerous waters or unknown lands. It would be helpful to have at least some rendering or course to follow. Without such a guide, we either won't get where we want to go or won't know where we are once we're there.

Sailing off into one's life without some sort of map to follow seems a lot like Columbus heading west and stabbing a flag into the beach of the Bahamas, thinking he was in India. Columbus's journey would have been much easier if he'd had an accurate map of the territory—one showing, for instance, that there was a whole continent between where he landed and where he thought he was.[1] Fortunately for us, however, many, many people have sailed these waters of life before us. Many have found meaning and fulfillment and, yes, even discovered their own specific life's mission. We can learn from them and chart our courses accordingly. That, in short, is the purpose of this book.

So what type of map can we construct to help us find the unique mission in each of our lives? The best maps tell us where we are, show us clearly where we want to go, and display the routes to get there. For an idea about how to do this, let's go back to Frankl. In one of the most profound paragraphs I've ever read anywhere, Frankl wrote:

> The opportunities to act properly, the potentialities to fulfill a meaning, are affected by the irreversibility of our lives....For as soon as we have used an opportunity and have actualized a potential meaning, we have done so once and for all. We have rescued it into the past wherein it has been safely delivered and deposited. In the past, nothing is irretrievably lost, but rather, on the contrary, everything is irrevocably stored and treasured. To be

---

[1] Of course, this would mean that someone else had been there before him and, consequently, that there would be no Columbus, Ohio—a situation to which those of us from Michigan might be able to adjust.

sure, people tend to see only the stubble fields of transitoriness but overlook and forget the full granaries of the past into which they have brought the harvest of their lives: the deeds done, the loves loved, and last but not least, the sufferings they have gone through with courage and dignity.

In other words, the past, present, and future are all equal entities! What a concept. If this is true, we can look at our lives as consisting of three states, all of which are equal in importance and relevance:

1. Potential (what will happen in the future)
2. Actualization (what we are doing in the present)
3. Legacy (what we have "rescued into the past")

Potential is the easy one. In fact, it's the condition upon which most of our modern society focuses. *New York Times* op-ed writer David Brooks wrote, "The unofficial religion of America is futurism." We focus on potential so much one might almost call us obsessive. We talk about our future, our potential, or upcoming opportunities, etc., etc. We talk about the importance of youth, the freshness of unlived days stretched out before us, and we get all misty-eyed. We emphasize education and credentials, preparation and training, all in the name of potential.

Actualization is, quite simply, where things become *actual*. Another term for actualization might be "doing." Actualization is the step in which we act upon our potentials and turn them into reality. In general, potential is more exciting than actualization because "doing" means—well, doing. And that means work. But this is where Frankl talks about finding and fulfilling one's life mission, one's true and unique purpose. We have no problem focusing on this phase either. It is an undeniable fact that we value an achievement orientation at the expense of almost everything else.

We lose our balance, however, when we get to legacy. Legacy is the sum total of all our actualizations. It represents the grand total accumulation of everything we have done, experienced, and lived. What blew me away about Frankl's classification of our individual legacy, to coin a clunky term, was its "artifactness." He didn't view the past as most of us do, as something dead and buried, over and done with, washed away in the draught. Rather, he saw it as a solid, undeniable reality. He represented it as being on an equal footing with our potential and our actions. This is huge when we consider how we should go about choosing what to do with our time because what he has suggested is that each passing moment (and what we choose to do with it) *matters*. It's not gone; it's transformed from potential into past by the actions we took toward it. Deep stuff.

As soon as I came to grips with Frankl's idea of the equality of future, present, and past, I pictured one pail pouring out our life's potential into another. The pouring pail is our Potential, the receiving pail our Legacy. The water flowing between the two represents our Actualization, or the living out of our potential in the present moment.

These three pieces together have almost given us the map we sought, although, to be sure, a diagram of a pair of pails is not nearly as cool as, say, a seventeenth-century pirate treasure map. But if one intelligently digs into the truths behind each of these symbols, the treasure available to its discoverer is more than anything ever hoarded by Edward Teach.[2]

However, there is one last feature to consider. Obviously, some of our potential goes unrealized. We don't actualize everything into our legacy, as most certainly, we waste some of it. In reality,

---

[2] The infamous Blackbeard.

INTRODUCTION

we waste quite a large portion of it. In fact, we ought to aspire, as one of our chief goals, to be the best stewards we possibly can with this potential. After all, it's entirely a gift. So for the sake of completing the treasure map (okay, diagram), let's add the loss or waste of our potential as *Spillage*.

There.

Now what have we got?

A really bizarre acronym, for one. **PAiLS = Potential and Actualization into Legacy and Spillage.** More seriously, we've got a framework or a simple map for the territory of our lives.

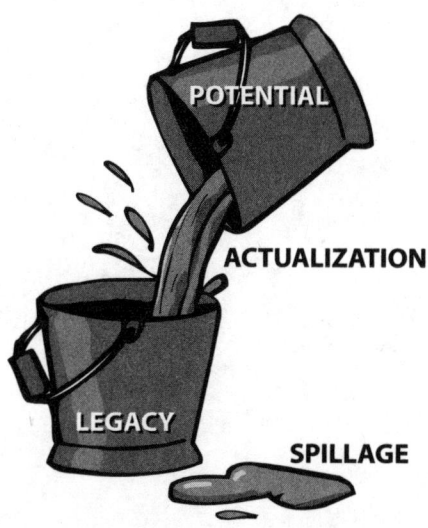

Using this basic diagram, we can begin to answer the question of how to take Gandalf's advice and make the most out of the time we've been given. Even now, as time ticks off the clock, our potential is flowing into our legacy.

Potential

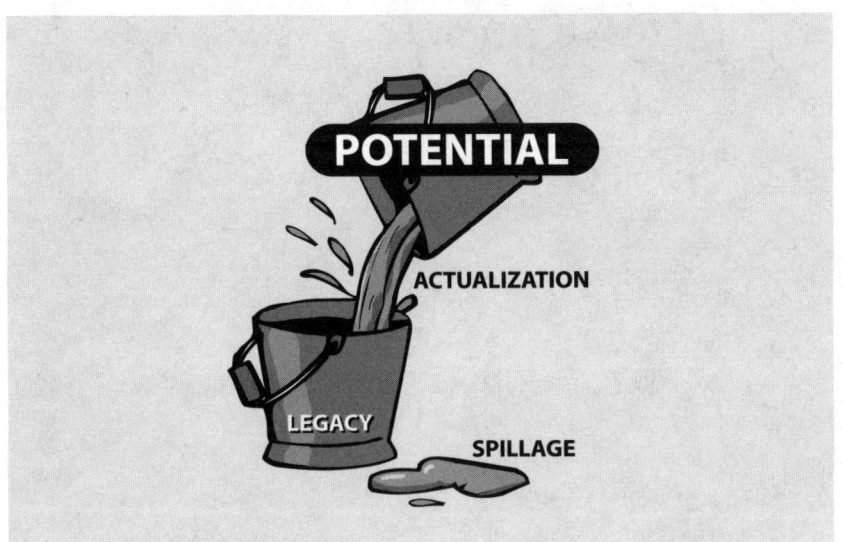

What Will You Do?

– 1 –
Monument

When we first moved to North Carolina, our real estate agent informed us that our street dead-ends into John Grisham's wife's horse farm. My wife Terri and I found this worthless bit of trivia charming, as we've got a long history with John Grisham (though he doesn't know it). You see, in our dating years, one of our favorite pastimes was to read Grisham's novels aloud to each other. Well, okay, not exactly. Terri would read them aloud to me. We did this in the car, at the park, and on the deck of the low-budget cruise we took on our honeymoon. Grisham's books had only been out for a few years at the time we first discovered them.

Fast forward to a year ago. Somehow an article about John Grisham and baseball fields came to my attention. Evidently, Grisham's biggest dream as a thirteen-year-old boy was to become a professional baseball player. This has translated itself into a portion of his philanthropy. Grisham, who famously left his career as an attorney to write tightly wound legal thrillers, has apparently begun building baseball parks for kids. "There was nowhere around here for kids to play baseball," Grisham said. What resulted was an elaborate park of six meticulous fields and a sign prohibiting profanity. Conspicuous by its absence, however, is the sign indicating the name of the park's patron. Grisham didn't want recognition for building the park.

Additionally, Grisham is a big contributor to the post–Hurricane Katrina fund called Rebuild the Coast. He also funds a scholarship for southern writers at Mississippi University, as well as supporting the Democratic Party.[1] In fact, Grisham's philanthropy is extensive enough that it can almost be seen as a third *phase* of his life. And this observation, in particular, is what I took from the article.

It immediately occurred to me that other well-known figures have lived out their lives in phases as well. Consider Benjamin Franklin.[2] The first phase of his life was being a young printer's apprentice. He used this opportunity wisely, honing not only his printing skills but also a growing acumen as both a writer and a businessman. These he grew into a business empire that would provide him an ongoing passive income sufficient to allow him to shift into his next phase: becoming a natural scientist.

It was the Age of Curiosity, and gentlemen everywhere were becoming self-taught experts on everything from botany and bugs to, yes, electricity. This was, to be sure, Franklin's passion. He even accepted a post as ambassador to England on behalf of first Pennsylvania and then later other colonies so that he could commingle with his peers in the prestigious Royal Society of Arts, becoming its first international member.

It wasn't until a pesky little interruption called the American Revolutionary War dawned (which Franklin would be slow to understand and join) that his scientific career took a backseat to the next and final phase of his life: statesmanship. Franklin would go on to be instrumental in obtaining French aid for the war (and thereby victory) and one of the only men to sign the Declaration of Independence, the Treaty of Paris, and the Constitution of the United States.

---

1 Apparently he is a distant cousin to Bill Clinton. Who knew?
2 Who seems to show up in every book I ever write because he can't resist being a great illustration of just about everything.

So here are two men, one legendary and one contemporary, who both seem to have lived out their lives in phases. One might more accurately say *layers* because phases seem to suggest that they were final once experienced, but layers are more in keeping with Frankl's idea of the past being still in existence. In fact, looking at our life in layers turns out to be one of the keys to unlocking an age-old conflict of advice on how to live one's life.

Conflicting Advice

My mother's parents struggled to raise a young family through the Depression. They had their final child during World War II, twelve years after they thought they were out of the childbearing business. To this daughter, my mother, they recommended becoming a nurse because she would "always have a job." This advice was entirely true and extremely pragmatic. My mother was employed most of her adult life, just as they'd predicted. But even though she identified with the nurturing and caring aspects of the profession, she was rarely thrilled with her occupation overall. As most know, nursing is an extremely challenging career, requiring a combination of technical knowledge and medical proficiency paired with manual labor, as well as the ability to handle disgusting (my kids would say "gross") situations, relatively low wages (although I have been told this is changing), and horrendous hours with inconvenient shifts.[3] What's more, she always wondered what other avenues might have been open to her but were left unexplored merely because she never really was encouraged to look for them.

A set of my cousins received almost the exact opposite advice. They were told to "follow their hearts" and "do what they love." As a result, they obtained college degrees in obscure fields and

---
[3] My brother and I still tease our dad about all the cube-steak and baked-bean dinners he prepared while our mom worked second shift!

then were forced by necessity to live out their lives in low-paying menial jobs entirely unrelated to their interests or training.

Here we see two very different, even polar opposite philosophies regarding the route to success. The results given in these specific cases are in no way all-inclusive, however. There are certainly people who have pursued pragmatic occupations and found perfect contentment in them. Others, obviously, have successfully pursued their passions. However, stories of success or failure in each category do not clear up the conflict.

When I ask intelligent, well-adjusted, successful people what advice they give their children about how to choose their life's work, I get everything from blank stares to empty platitudes that all run together like the undecipherable voices of Charlie Brown's parents. Usually, I press further, relating the two distinct paths just described and asking which they recommend. What usually comes out is that education gets big approval, followed by the extremely popular wish that "I just want my children to be happy." The result of this kind of fuzzy entrance ramp onto the highway of productive life is millions of kids heading to college merely because it's the thing to do, followed by millions of young adults working jobs that don't fulfill them, followed by millions of middle-aged people feeling frustrated and "stuck," followed by millions of older people full of bitterness and regret.

I was attending a leadership conference once when one of the keynote speakers passionately launched into the following: "What is the secret to success? I'll tell you! The secret to success is to fall down 99 times and get up 100!" At this bit of motivational wisdom, the crowd went wild. Everyone seemed inspired to go out and change the world right then and there. And good for them. However, this little statement amused me to no end. There are many things that sound good on first hearing but fall apart upon analysis.[4] This statement in particular can only be motivational to people who are bad at math. Just how, exactly, does a person get up one more time than he or she has fallen down? It's impossible.

In this same class, I place the two opposite pieces of life advice introduced above. "Pursue a career solely for the sake of pragmatism and security" and "Do what you love, and the money will follow" are equally misleading. While there may be elements of truth and even wisdom contained in each (more on this later), they are both patently untrue on their face. The real problem is that the two look like different and separate paths. They are not.

Life as a Ziggurat

In the Bible, we are told of the early humans building a tower in Babylon in defiance of their Creator. Their goal was to demonstrate their autonomy by erecting a monument to their own glory as high as the sky. God decided to smack them down from this lofty pride by destroying their tower and confounding their common language into many different ones, and ever since, we've had guidance counselors everywhere recommending four years of a foreign language.[5]

Historians seem quite sure that the structure these early builders made was a type of pyramid called a ziggurat. A ziggurat is made up of stepped layers. Each progressive layer upward is smaller than the one below. For instance, here is a ziggurat comprised of four layers:

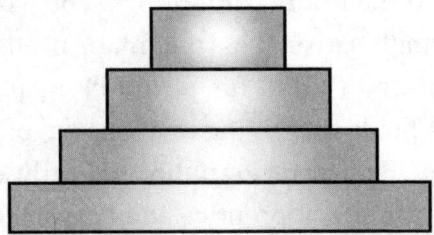

---

4 Perhaps even this book.
5 Allow me to recommend Italian.

Okay, upon further consideration, this looks more like a layer cake, but you get the idea.

One of the key insights to help us reconcile the opposing life advice described above is this: ***Our lives are not choices along different paths so much as a stack of layers.*** If everything we do is still part of us, then as we live through the days of our lives, we are adding each day to our monument. As we saw in the examples of John Grisham and Benjamin Franklin, their lives were lived out in phases or layers. For instance, John Grisham's ziggurat would look something like the figure shown below.

> *Our lives are not choices along different paths so much as a stack of layers.*

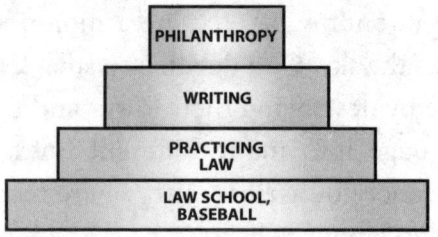

His early experiences were dreams of playing professional baseball, followed by a college education and then a law degree. For his pragmatic occupation, he practiced law, while he pursued his passion of writing by waking early and putting his first manuscript together in the hours before work. His passionate pursuit of writing eventually satisfied his pragmatic needs and ultimately gave him resources to fulfill his purposeful calling of building anonymous ball fields and giving to a long list of other causes.

In the case of Benjamin Franklin, his early experiences included being a printer's apprentice and bit writer for *Poor Richard's Almanac*. This gave him experience in running a business and working hard. His pragmatic occupation became print-shop ownership and franchising (as well as residential rental properties and government salaries—he was postmaster general of Philadelphia, for instance). The success of his pragmatic occupation supported his many passions and curiosities, allowing him to invent and discover a staggering diversity of things. Finally, these passions, which had made him famous, opened doors for him to become a statesman and perform matchless service for his country.

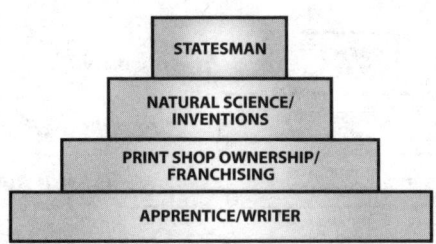

We can learn a lot from the layers lived by these two men about how to construct our own lives.

Notice that the lowest layer consists of our *preparatory experiences*. These include our education (formal and otherwise), mistakes, missteps, misadventures, histories, hobbies, early interests, associations, relationships, and everything and anything that contributes to our development. Of this layer, we can say, "It happened to me."

Stacked upon this foundation is our *pragmatic occupation*. This represents whatever we find to do that works effectively to support us financially. Of this layer, we say, "It feeds me."

Next comes the layer that represents our *passions*. These are the things for which our heart yearns, the activities for which we show a natural affinity, the pursuits in which we long to involve ourselves. Here is where our natural talents shine through. Here is where we say, "It fulfills me." These activities make us feel the most authentic.

Finally, at the top comes our *purposeful calling*. This is the highest order of our actualization. It is where we maximize our role as contributors to society and as human beings. By the way, "purposeful" nearly always means "other-focused." It is when we are giving and serving others that we really see a purpose beyond our own myopic self-interest. It is of this level that we say, "It is my duty." This level is where we feel the most alive, most useful, and most in line with the highest picture we hold of ourselves.

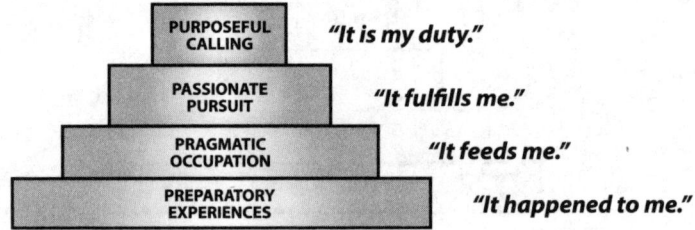

Understanding the Layers

The first thing to understand about this ziggurat (or layer cake) of our lives is that *all four layers are required in order to maximize our happiness.* Those people who have built up robust layers at each level are the ones who tend to be the most content, the most fulfilled, and yes, the happiest. Happiness is not something that can be obtained by direct pursuit; rather, it's the side effect of a life rightly lived. And a life rightly lived will consistently involve all four levels of this diagram.

> **Happiness is not something that can be obtained by direct pursuit; rather, it's the side effect of a life rightly lived.**

While most of us fumble upward, building our ziggurats one mud brick at a time, every now and then, someone seems to bypass a layer or two and shoot directly upward. Consider singer Justin Bieber, for instance. How much preliminary experience could he really have had to become a wildly popular entertainer, pursuing his passion from a young age? It is from examples like his that people are tempted to say things such as "Just follow your heart, and the money will come." But we must remember that the Justin Biebers of this world are the exception.

Another example is preachers or ministers. They often refer to their entrance into their life's work as a "calling." They were headed in one self-determined direction one day, and then God got ahold of them the next, calling them to a life of service to Him. Ask any of them, and this is the language you will hear. In their case, with a call straight from God, they were given a pass directly to the top of the ziggurat.

Even for all the Justin Biebers and pastors out there, the entire stack must still be built for them to maximize their potential. Consider what would happen to Justin Bieber if he never allowed himself to feel and respond to a purposeful calling. All his money and fame would leave him empty and narcissistic if he didn't find a way to pour himself into something higher than himself. Or what about the preachers—or doctors or teachers or any others who feel a definite "call" to do what they do? If they do not find a way to support their calling with passion—worse, if they cannot succeed in finding a way for it to pay the bills and be a pragmatic support—the call itself will go largely unrealized. From this, we can see that, even in the case of those rare individuals who appear to begin a layer or two above the rest of us mere mortals, they too must follow the instructions and assemble a complete monument out of their life. To do otherwise leaves one incomplete.

Speaking of incomplete, what of the person who goes no higher than a pragmatic occupation? Have you ever been around anyone like that? They have no interest beyond merely paying the bills, coming home from work, and mindlessly turning on the television or video games. Their life is empty of passion and becomes the saddest kind of self-imposed servitude.

What of the person who goes no higher than passions? Take the person who holds down a nice pragmatic occupation and then pours his passion into sports or hobbies or any number of ultimately meaningless distractions. Again, without directing our passions upward (even if they are meaningful ones) in the pursuit of a purposeful calling, we remain empty and self-focused. This never leads to lasting happiness, and the contributions that might have been made go wasted.

It is worth repeating: ***all four layers of the ziggurat are required to maximize one's potential, fulfillment, and happiness.***

The Fallacy of Arrival

Additionally, it can be seen from this stack of layers that in life, there is no arrival. Life is a journey that we take, and that journey is an accumulation of experiences and achievements and contributions. Many people seem to feel as if their life would be complete "if only" they could:

- Find their perfect mate
- Land that particular job
- Get a college degree
- Win that certain scholarship
- Hit their target weight
- Make it to retirement
- Earn a million dollars

The list could go on indefinitely. None of these things are the defining pinnacles of our lives. None of them has the ability to bring final and lasting happiness. While many of them are desirable and even important, our lives are much more than "event fulfillment." Instead, our lives are monuments built one second at a time, stack upon stack of experiences and contributions and thoughts and moments.

Our goal should be to make as beautiful a stack of these layers as we possibly can. That means filling the foundational layer with all sorts of broad and meaningful experiences; even mistakes and missteps can be constructive when considered as merely stepping stones upward. When we find something that works pragmatically, it is meaningless unless it feeds our passions. In turn, our passions ring hollow if they don't then enable us to fulfill a higher purpose. We need all the layers, and we should add to them consistently.

This is why some of the happiest, most productive people never stop or retire. They are too fulfilled strengthening and adding to the layers of their lives. They know that they are not done leaving their legacy until the last drop of their potential has poured from their pail.

The message is to consider your life as a monument you build—not, as the early Babylonians, in defiance of the Creator, but rather in thankfulness to Him. It has been said that your life is a gift from God; what you do with it is your gift back to Him. So build it accordingly.

> **Your life is a gift from God; what you do with it is your gift back to Him.**

– 2 –
Place

One of my favorite movies of all time is *The Legend of Bagger Vance*, written by Steven Pressfield and directed and produced by Robert Redford. Not that I'm much of a golfer (or a golfer at all, in fact), but the plot, acting, and cinematography are excellent. The reason it is so memorable, however, is because of the message it delivers.

The premise is that a young man, who was a gifted golfer as a youth, went to World War I and came back messed up. He couldn't golf anymore, feeling responsible for the death of his comrades and unable to clear his head. Ten years later, a mysterious caddy named Bagger Vance appears to help him work through his challenges. The young man, called Captain Junuh, says he has lost his swing. Bagger Vance shows him what an authentic swing is by referring him to his competitors. Although these men have radically different playing styles, they are both effective at the game because each plays it in his own unique way, doing what he was born to do in the way he was born to do it.

Captain Junuh goes through many ups and downs during the big three-day tournament. Sometimes he catches a break and does well for a while, but then his reaction to it is arrogance and cockiness. Then he messes up horribly and loses confidence, whining that he shouldn't be playing at all. From extreme to extreme, he goes. Finally, when it is almost too late for Captain Junuh to have a chance in the competition, Bagger Vance pulls him aside and says, "It's time." Junuh resists at first, but Bagger Vance presses the point, telling Junuh that it is time to move on with his life, time to drop the baggage of the past, time to find his authentic swing and do what he was born to do in the way he was made to do it.

If Viktor Frankl was right, each of us, like Captain Junuh, has an authentic swing deep down inside. All we have to do is discover it.

The Ziggurat Resolves the Conflict

We are now ready to fully address the conflicting life advice discussed in the previous chapter. You'll remember that one line of reasoning was to find something that works financially, whether you find the work fulfilling or not, because at least you'll always have security. The other camp said to follow your heart and do what you love, and the money will follow. One side seems to promise security without fulfillment, while the other offers fulfillment without security. We can make sense of this by returning to the ziggurat diagram.

> **One side seems to promise security without fulfillment, while the other offers fulfillment without security.**

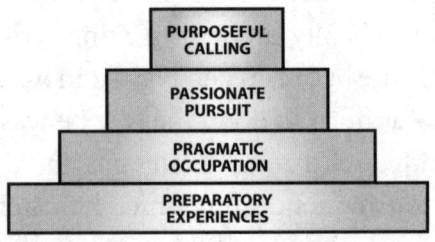

Step one is to start all the way at the top. Stephen Covey famously taught to "begin with the end in mind." This means we should take a look at our lives as if from our deathbed, looking back on all we've done. Coming back into the present, we should then make our decisions based upon that perspective. Some people have also called this the "tombstone test" because it effectively means to consider your life as though it's over and make sure you do today what you'll wish you had done then.

This is all very helpful advice. But here I would like to offer a slight tweak. Instead of considering your life as a timeline with an ending, let's stick with the layers concept and use the ziggurat diagram to do it in a slightly different way. Let's begin with your highest purpose in mind, meaning, consider what calling you have or the highest contribution you would like to make. Do you have one? Do you feel a special call? Do you have a yearning to contribute in a certain area? If you do, then we next move down to the layer below it to passionate pursuits.

What passions do you have that support that higher purpose? What things do you do that fulfill you, that you show an amazing affinity for, and for which people affirm you and give you rave reviews? Next, we consider pragmatic steps that support those passions. What types of occupations allow you to do the things that you are passionate about? Consider the whole wide range that is available. Finally, working our way down to the foundational level, we can then begin constructing experiences and putting in place the correct education and preparation to support the structure we have considered from the top down.

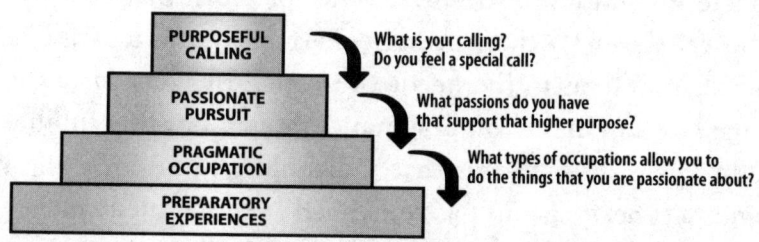

Perhaps some examples will clarify.

Let's imagine a teenage boy who aspires to serve the Lord and bring Him glory with his life. For now, that's as clear a calling or purpose as the young boy can express. That is the top layer of his ziggurat. What then should we tell the boy about how to live his life? The answer is to follow the progression we just worked through above.

We should tell that boy to next consider the things he is passionate about. Let's say his dream is to play soccer as a professional, and he feels that by doing so, he could be a strong public example for his religious faith (Tim Tebow–style) and thereby fulfill his ultimate calling. Excellent. The soccer playing is the next layer down in his ziggurat, the layer called Passionate Pursuit.

Pragmatically, though, one cannot know if this young boy will really be able to make it as a professional soccer player. The odds are certainly against it, for one thing. But remember that the pragmatic layer is much larger than the passionate layer. This is for a reason. There are many ways in which the boy's passion for the game of soccer can lead to pragmatic success. For instance, he could go into coaching. He could go into sports administration or management. He could become a sports marketer or a sports agent. He could even become a sports statistician or sports therapist.

It is here that we must again consider the layer above, the Passionate Pursuit level. Are there other passions that the boy can identify? Certainly there must be. Perhaps he has a caring heart and likes to tend to the needs of people. By considering these things, we can dial in on pragmatic occupations that fulfill each of these passions. In this case, he could go into anything that combines these various passions, such as sports medicine.

Finally, we drop down to the lowest layer, Preparatory Experiences. It is here that we can determine which experiences, which educational choices, and what activities the boy should be immediately pursuing. Are there certain individuals in the sports world to whom we can introduce the boy? Are there colleges that will offer the boy a chance to play on their soccer team that also offer degrees that align with some of these areas? It can be seen that by beginning at the top, at the boy's highest purpose, and working downward, we can send the boy off in a direction that will at least serve his passions and produce a wide range of possible pragmatic occupations in that same category. It cannot be known exactly where all this will take him, but the *direction* will be correct.

This very simple example demonstrates how we don't have to send the boy down one wrong path or another (security on one side or fulfillment on the other). Instead, we can work "top down" from his slightest detections of an overall purpose, through his known passions, right down to the most practical steps he can take now.

Let's look at another example. A young girl is not sure of any overall purpose or calling and therefore has no idea about that top layer of her ziggurat. It's too fuzzy at this point. That's fine. In fact, it's probably this way for most people, especially those of the younger set. All we need do in such an instance is drop down to the next level at which she shows some bit of self-knowledge. Let's say it's at the level of Passionate Pursuit. She enjoys playing the piano and singing. In fact, she loves everything about music. Let's also say that she has a passion for gathering people together and hosting events.

Equipped with these insights, we drop down to the Pragmatic Occupation level and brainstorm everything that might support these passions. One clear consideration is that she could play music as a professional. All the various ways (concert bands, symphonies, pop bands, as a solo recording artist, songwriter, etc.) should be considered. Also, she may be able to teach music, either giving individual lessons or as a teacher in a school or collegiate setting. But her enjoyment of people and hosting events might suggest that she could become a promoter or an agent. In this way, we see that there are many possible careers that are in line with all of her passions.

Finally, we drop down to the level of Preparatory Experiences to begin arranging for the correct experiences and education. What music lessons can she take? Are there people in some of the professions above to whom we can introduce her? Are there colleges or music schools that offer formal training in these areas? The broader she can make the base of her preparatory experiences in direct support of her known passions, the better.

So in the case of an individual without a sense of an overall purpose, we can work our way downward from the Passionate Pursuit layer of the ziggurat all the way to steps the girl can take right now. Nothing is rigidly determined except a direction that aligns her passions with possible pragmatic choices and the correct underpinning of experience and education.

Next, let's consider an individual who shows no real indication of significant passions and is therefore unsure about the top two layers of his ziggurat. Can we begin as far down as the pragmatic layer and still determine a proper course? Yes. We do so by considering the natural affinities and skills such a person displays. There are many great works available on skills-based analysis and determining what a person is good at. Some researchers break strengths down into different categories; others use testing methods to determine skills.

Really, though, it doesn't have to be complicated. A person's natural skills and affinities are often readily apparent. One can determine these by asking simple questions. Is he good with his hands? With machinery? With tools? Can he think spatially and understand diagrams? Then we must search for occupational situations in which these skills are in demand. Then it's an easy step to determine which educational or vocational training arrangements should therefore be made in preparation.

How Did I Get Here, and Where Am I Going?

So far, we've considered three examples of young people with most of their lives still ahead of them. But what about the rest of us? What about the millions of people not happy with their current life? Simple. This exercise will apply not only to young people just beginning their adult lives but also to the rest of us somewhere between the beginning and the end. While there will certainly be a time when it's "too late," most likely that time has not come yet. You can still add experiences and activities to your ziggurat layers that are part of your "authentic swing." Remember, if we go back to the diagram of the pails in the introduction, every drop of your potential has the chance to become part of your legacy—right up to and including the last one.

> **Every drop of your potential has the chance to become part of your legacy—right up to and including the last one.**

Now, to be sure, we cannot ever get rid of any part of the ziggurat we've been constructing our entire lives. It's all there, it's all a part of us, and it's all part of our legacy. But we *can* always make it better by working a "top down" strategy to determine a correct direction for ourselves based upon our highest callings and our truest passions. It's the best way to determine what to do with the time that has been given us, or for many of us, the time we have remaining.

The way to begin this is to think about and write down the layers of your own personal ziggurat to this point in your life. In other words, what does your personal ziggurat look like right now? Fill in each layer of the diagram below. This is a very constructive exercise. It will do a lot to help explain how you got to where you are in life. It should make sense of all the crazy experiences and "failures" you've gone through so far. Properly considered, each of these has become part of what makes you unique.

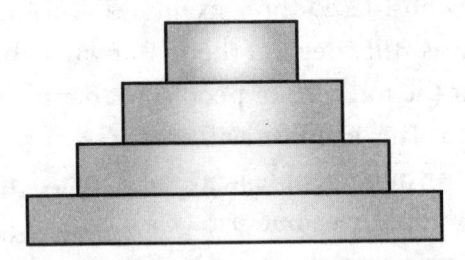

Overall, how does your ziggurat look? Does it have all four levels? If not, you have identified one huge part of what needs to be done—and probably provided a reason for any feeling of unfulfilled potential you may have in your life. Remember, we need all four layers to maximize our potential and feel the most fulfilled.

Are any of your layers lacking in some way? If so, the layers above may really be suffering. If a lower layer is not strong, there is no way it can support much above it. For instance, perhaps your passions are really lacking. This will certainly inhibit your ability to serve a larger purpose, as purposeful living is nothing if not passionate. In another possible scenario, if you are struggling to make it financially (meaning that your Pragmatic Occupation is weak) then you are going to have a difficult time focusing on your passions and how they might serve a higher purpose. Under such conditions, you are likely just trying to survive. Or let's consider the case in which your Preparatory Experiences are not very strong. This in turn is limiting your ability to find a Pragmatic Occupation that really works. In such a case, it would mean pursuing more education or training to build a bigger base upon which to put a more successful occupation.

So now that you have taken stock of where you are, it's time to consider where you'd like to go. If you don't have all four layers, or if some of your layers are insufficient, fixing this is your immediate task. Maybe you do have all four layers, but they just don't add up to what you want; then you also need to make a change. As the saying goes, "If you want to see some changes in your life, you're going to have to make some changes in your life."

Just as in the examples of the young people above, you should take the same approach. Work from the top down. Draw out your ziggurat the way you'd *like* it to be. What calling or purpose do you want your life's monument to serve? What overall contribution can you make with the stack of experiences and achievements you've assembled so far?

It helps to focus at the top, on an overall life purpose and calling. Remember, Viktor Frankl taught us that this is man's highest priority. Now working downward, try to identify what your dominant passions are that could support that overall goal. Next (and by now this should be becoming familiar), figure out what you can still do with where you are in your pragmatic occupation to be in line with those passions and pointing upward toward your bigger purpose. Is a change in your occupation necessary? Is it a lateral move you can make without too much shakeup to your current status, or does it require a more significant change? The bigger the change required, the more courage you will need in order to do it. Perhaps you could be like John Grisham and pursue your passion in off-work hours until it becomes successful enough to replace your current Pragmatic Occupation.

The possibilities and combinations are endless. The key is that using the ziggurat to work a top-down approach gives you direction and makes use of all your passions and abilities. In effect, it can get you "unstuck" and moving onward toward your life's highest meaning and fulfillment.

Turning Points

All this is not to say that you are constructing a rigid course that cannot be adjusted. The exercise of using the ziggurat to determine a direction is flexible. It is likely that, at the top, the higher purpose won't change much, but the farther down you go in the layers, the more things will probably morph as time goes by.

In Act IV, Scene 3 of Shakespeare's *Julius Caesar*, Brutus famously says:

> There is a tide in the affairs of men
> Which, taken at the flood, leads on to fortune;
> Omitted, all the voyage of their life
> Is bound in shallows and in miseries.
> On such a full sea we are now afloat,
> And we must take the current when it serves,
> Or lose our ventures.

This is a good reminder that there are key moments in our lives in which opportunities present themselves. We need to be sure to grab hold of them when they come along, or we might run the risk of being "bound in shallows and miseries."

How do we know which opportunities to take and which to let pass by? Certainly there will be many things that come along that are *good* but not *great*. What may be the perfect opportunity for one individual may not be for another. This is why blanket prescriptions such as "Go to school, get good grades, and get a good, secure job" are so misleading. Again, our ziggurat diagram can help.

In each and every case, all we need do is compare the opportunity to the layers of our ziggurat. Does the opportunity fit with our highest purpose, or is it merely a distraction? Does it align with our passions and add to what we feel fulfilled doing, or does it not exactly fit? Again, we can use each of the layers and where we would ultimately like to take them to determine whether something that comes along is *for* us or not.

When I was an undergraduate engineering student, I learned of a scholarship program for graduate school that appealed to me. In the first place, it made obtaining a master's degree financially possible. Second, it allowed me to do so immediately upon completion of my undergraduate degree. So early in my college years, I set a goal to win this scholarship and attend a particular school. I worked hard, kept my eye on the prize, and ultimately was able to obtain the scholarship.

To do so, however, I had to apply to three different graduate schools. The particular engineering degree for which I was aiming was a bit obscure, so I dug around in a book of colleges in the library and hurriedly put down two alternate choices. Never would I have predicted what would happen next. Somehow, over the course of the application process, I changed my mind. The school I had dreamed of attending all those years, which had accepted me, was cast aside. I chose one of the alternates instead. I had never even visited the campus! I was attracted to this particular university because I had learned they were sending students overseas to complete their graduate thesis work. This appealed to me immensely. In addition, this school was much closer to home, and somehow I took comfort in that. No doubt there were other reasons, but I can't remember them now.

This little change in direction became a major turning point in my life. As a result of attending that school, I met my wife. Further, after completing my degree, I returned to my hometown and became associated with some colleagues who would become not only lifelong friends but long-term business partners as well. None of this ever would have happened in that exact way had I gone to the original school.

Any of us who have lived a number of years can likely point to turning points in our lives similar to this. However, it is just as likely that there have been very few of them. Turning points of this magnitude are as important as they are rare. How can we know which ones to take "at the flood" and which ones to let pass by? Again, if we are in tune with the layers of our ziggurat diagram, we can have some sense of security that we are choosing correctly.

Of course, no one can know for sure. Choices come along, and we do the best we can. But working backward from our highest purpose downward is a sure bet that we won't choose something that will lead us astray. Even my sudden change in direction was still in keeping with my passions and overall direction. As a result, it became an enormous portion of my Preparatory Experiences that has led me to where I am today (wherever that is).

It's Your Life

Remember that it's *your* life. Only you can live the life that God alone has called you to live. Only you can fulfill your particular destiny and higher purpose. Sooner or later, you've got to get after what it is you were put here to do, or you'll suffer miserably for knowing that you're not doing it. It will haunt you in the quiet hours of your days. It will whisper to you in the dark of the night. It will not leave you alone until it's truly too late. And rest assured; there *is* a too late. There is another incorrect motivational phrase to go along with "fall down 99 times and get up 100;" it's the one that says, "It's never too late." There most certainly *is* a "too late." There always is. It's just not *yet*. It's not too late *yet*.

> **Sooner or later, you've got to get after what it is you were put here to do, or you'll suffer miserably for knowing that you're not doing it.**

It is supremely important to treat your life as a journey of discovery. You are unearthing your highest calling and deepest purpose. Many, many of us don't have much of an idea of this until we've lived for a long time. That's okay. If we head in the direction indicated by our ziggurat, we'll at least be on the right track. We'll make self-discoveries along the way. We have been gifted this life, our bodies, our mind and soul, our abilities, talents, and temperaments. The game is to learn about who we are, what we have been given, and how we are made and to unearth—gradually, step by step—what we are supposed to do and who we are supposed to become.

Don't look for a field to go into; instead, look for a direction to *thrill* to. It is a grand adventure. It is a building project like no other. And it is yours alone. Only do what only you can do, and do it like no other because never has there been, nor ever will there be, another like you. Your place in this world is an address that only you can occupy.

> **Don't look for a field to go into; instead, look for a direction to *thrill* to.**

Actualization

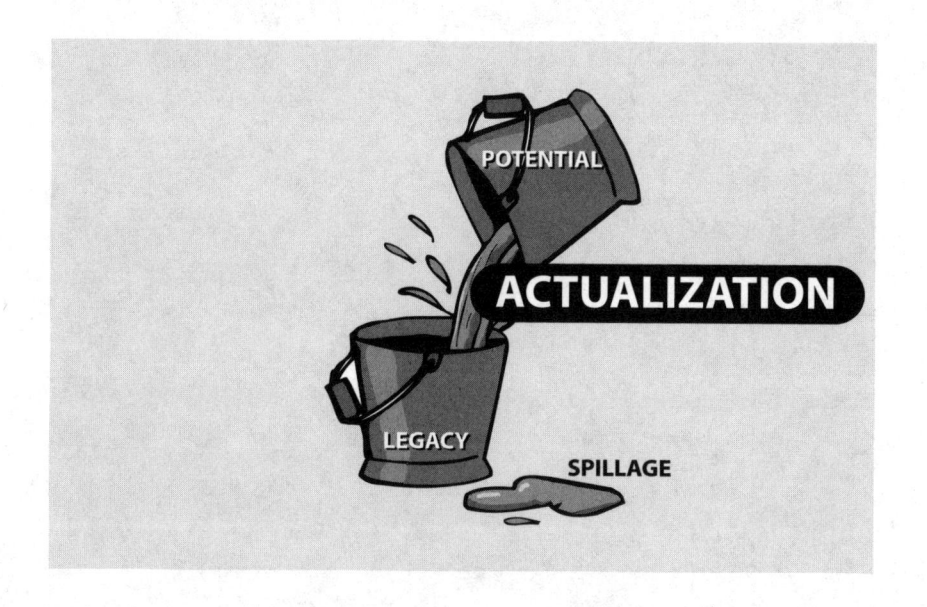

How Will You Do It?

– 3 –
Difficulty

Guy Kawasaki wrote, "Success takes crazy, passionate people who believe they can change the world." Tim McGraw sings, "How bad do you want it? How bad do you need it? Are you eatin', sleepin', dreamin' with that one thing on your mind?… 'Cause if you want it all, you've got to lay it all out on the line." Each of these suggests that there is something a little over the top about success. Statistics appear to prove them right.

Consider the average new business success rate of only 50 percent after the first five years, with just 35 percent of those businesses even being around in the tenth year. In fact, most of these never make any money at all in their first decade but instead barely pay off original investors.

How about the small percentages of school athletes who make it to the professional level? Just six out of 1,000 high school baseball players will make it to the major leagues, or just 11.6 percent of college players. In football it's even worse, with just eight high school players out of 10,000 finding their way to the NFL, or just 1.7 percent of college players. The odds are similar in hockey, basketball, and soccer. Even more discouraging is the average career span of professional players. For baseball, it's 5.6 years, for basketball, 4.8 years, and for football, just 3.5 years. Long odds and short careers.

Actualization

So business seems tough. Sports seem tough. How about another category? Take writing books. Of the roughly one million titles published each year, a mere 200 or so go over the 100,000 copies sold mark. That's two out of 10,000.

What about acting? Who wouldn't want to be a movie star and get his or her name up in lights? Apparently only about 2 percent of those who claim to be working in the field can make a full-time living at it.

Let's get away from careers then as a measure of success. Let's look at something totally different—say, marriage. According to divorce and marriage expert Marty Friedman, 50 percent of first marriages end in divorce, and 60–70 percent of second marriages do. And the results of this dismal success rate are depressing: fatherless households account for 63 percent of youth suicides, 90 percent of homeless/runaways, 85 percent of behavioral problems, and 71 percent of high school dropouts.

What of goal setting in general? How do people do hitting goals they set for themselves? Unfortunately, the numbers don't improve much here either. According to researcher Douglas Vermeeren, 80 percent of people never even set goals. But of those who do, approximately 70 percent fail to hit them.

Often students will go off to college and complain that their curriculum is hard. Or individuals will start a new business and complain that success seems almost impossible. People everywhere will readily tell you how difficult it is to have a good marriage. Disillusionment and frustration always follow shortly after the collision of dreams with reality. The truth of the matter is that success everywhere, in anything, is extremely difficult. Finding excellence, excelling at what one does, and "making it" are not automatic or easy.

Often people mistakenly believe the difficulty of a task is the fault of the task itself. For instance, the college student who complains about his or her curriculum might conclude that it is simply a challenging curriculum. While this may be true, there is often more to the story. What the college student may not realize is that the curriculum is merely a representation of the success process in general. It's easy to blame the curriculum when, in actuality, it's *success itself* that is difficult.

The laws of success are brutal, cold-hearted, and consistent. When people bump against them, they tend to blame the specific instrument teaching them the lesson instead of realizing the deeper lesson itself. It's the age-old mistake of shooting the messenger because one doesn't like the message. Remember: Success, *true success*, anywhere and in anything, is difficult; otherwise it wouldn't be success. So don't worry when you run up against difficulty because it is normal. More than that, it's even good for us.

Trout Fisherman in Hell

There is an old story about a fisherman who believes he has died and gone to heaven as he catches one perfect two-pound trout after another. As he sets his fly and hooks into yet one more, he can't fathom his good fortune. The sky is blue, the weather ideal, the fish are biting like never before, and everything is absolutely perfect. It is not long, however, before the realization dawns on him that he is not in heaven at all. Instead, as the boredom and pointlessness settle in on him, he realizes he's actually in *hell*.

It's hard to describe just how hard this little parable hit me the first time I read it. I was blown away by the concept that if every little thing were absolutely perfect, the overall situation would *not* be. In one moment, this realization erased all my whiny complaints about how difficult and elusive success seems to be. The trout fisherman in hell story is so extreme, so seemingly ridiculous,

Without the struggle, we would feel no joy in victory at all.

that we are confronted with a strange and puzzling fact: We may hate opposition and struggle, but they are critical for our mental health. Without the struggle, we would feel no joy in victory at all.

How can this be? How can it be true that we are actually happier and more fulfilled when overcoming opposition than when everything is easy and simply rolling our way? It is because of the way we were made. Without a battle to win and an enemy to vanquish, the value of the warrior goes to zero. In the famous words of Thomas Paine, "What we attain too cheaply we esteem too lightly." In other words, if we don't earn it, we can't enjoy it.

This is profound, and it ought to provide a telling answer against all those dismal statistics above. If we consider only statistics and the "odds of success," most of us would never get out of bed in the morning, much less find a way to force ourselves to study for that upcoming calculus exam or go after that higher-level certification for our job. You see, it doesn't matter how difficult success is or what the odds are of making it. What matters is our struggle against the opposition, the force of our will against the force of everything that would try and stop us.

Not only does it fulfill us to have something against which to push, but the process also makes us better. It is the resistive weight that builds the muscles. So ultimately, it doesn't matter whether success is hard. What matters is simply that we pursue it anyway.

The Blunt Realities of Success

Gaining the correct Preparatory Experiences, finding the right Pragmatic Occupation, Pursuing your Passions, and fulfilling your unique Purposeful Calling are going to depend largely upon how much you understand about success and how you think about what happens to you along your journey. It's one thing to construct an ideal ziggurat in the comfort of your imagination and dreams; it's another altogether to actualize it into reality with hard work over a lifetime. However, if you are truly building the correct ziggurat—one that matches all you are and all you were built to achieve—then much of it won't feel like work. In fact, you'll find that such work is more fun than fun. You will truly be able to pour yourself into the tasks at hand with enthusiasm because it is your "authentic swing."

However, even Captain Junuh had to learn how to think correctly about success in order to compete in the tournament. Therefore, let's consider ten realities of success. Having a realistic idea of what's headed your way is step one toward handling it with aplomb.

1. *You Will Work Your Butt Off.*

    Greatness requires sweat equity; there's no way around it. To attain greatness in any category will require that you push yourself—and hard at times. The flip side of this, however, is that at some point (and likely many points along the way), it will cease to feel like work and instead become more of a magnificent obsession. Again, this is why it is so important to map out the correct ziggurat so you don't work hard at something not in alignment with who you are and what you're supposed to accomplish. The hardest work in the world is the pointless kind. Think of a prison gang shoveling gravel on the side of the road (something I saw today while out riding my motorcycle)—not exactly the picture of a high work ethic.

    > **The hardest work in the world is the pointless kind.**

2. *You Will Feel like a Goof.*

Our society has fashioned an odd double-mindedness when it comes to success. Everybody wants to see the baby, but no one wants to hear about the labor pains. But success requires pressure and pain, and as we overcome resistance and opposition, there will inevitably be times when we ask ourselves, "Is this really what the successful ones did? They did *this*?"

I will never forget the early days of doing my part working on the rough draft of the manuscript for Orrin Woodward's and my first bestseller, *Launching a Leadership Revolution*. I was alone in my house, typing away, feeling like a total phony writing nonsense. Only later would I learn in talking to other authors that most of them have felt this way too, even sometimes after already having several successful books in the marketplace! The flip side of feeling like a goof is that eventually, if you stay at it long enough, you will feel like a champion.

3. *You Will Run into Knuckleheads.*

It's probably not totally nice to call other people names, but I have no other way to prepare you for what's coming without letting you know that they're out there. Truly. Even our friend Viktor Frankl wrote this: "There are two races of men in this world, but only these two—the 'race' of the decent man and the 'race' of the indecent man. Both are found everywhere. They penetrate into all groups of society." Jimmy Buffett sang it in a slightly more poignant manner: "Good times and riches and son of a _____es I've seen more than I can recall." The flip side of this is that you will also come across many wonderful people as well.

4. *You Will Doubt Yourself (and Just About Everything Else).*
    It's natural to have doubts along the way. You will be tempted to think you're not worthy of what you are pursuing or that the pursuit itself isn't worth the effort.

    This reminds me of the story of the boy who was being bullied out of his lunch money each day. To defend himself, he enrolled in a karate class. At the end of the first week of lessons, the instructor charged him fifteen dollars for his services. The boy promptly quit karate and decided it was easier to just keep paying the bully than to pay to learn how to fight him.

    This temptation will come to anyone who is truly in pursuit of excellence. Sometimes we will feel it is easier to pay the small daily price of mediocrity rather than the long-term price of excellence. The flip side is that eventually you will come to respect yourself for fighting through the doubts.

5. *You Will Have Reversals.*
    No one, however direct that person's path to success may look to outside observers, has ever made it in a straight line to his or her dreams. There are always setbacks and reversals along the way. This is unavoidable. It is okay to experience a failure now and again, as it is basically required. It is not okay to allow these failures to become final. In fact, a failure is never a true failure if it is not final. It is merely tuition for a lesson learned, which can then carry the striver forward. The flip side of this one is twofold: Obviously, with reversals will come

advances, too, if one just doesn't stop. Also, reversals have the secondary benefit of building character.

6. *Someone (or Several Someones) Will Preach to You.*

    Unsolicited advice is as common as the common cold and almost as unwelcome. For some reason, as soon as a person embarks upon a journey toward excellence, there are hordes who arrive at the dock to warn that "there be monsters in those waters." Some of this will be well-meant advice, while some of it will carry a whiff of jealousy or envy. Journey onward anyway, understanding that although some will preach, others will learn from you instead. Be a great example.

7. *You Will Have to Make a Million Unforeseen Adjustments.*

    Okay, a million is not a scientifically determined number here, but it does convey what it will feel like. Just as with the turning points described earlier, many smaller adjustments will be required. There is no way a sailor plotting a course can predict just how many movements of the rudder will be necessary to carry him to his destination. He just makes them as he goes, using his distant destination as his heading. Any journey toward excellence is the same. Be flexible and stay vigilant to the need for course corrections. Remember the formula Plan-Do-Check-Adjust (PDCA). Repeat it often and, where possible, with input from someone further along your journey than you.

8. *You Will Compare Yourself to Others.*

    Inevitably, in the course of your journey, you will be tempted to compare yourself to others. It may be that their path looks easier, their gifts better, or their destination nearer. Beware: Comparison is the root of all unhappiness. Remember all you've learned about your journey being uniquely and precisely your own. Embrace who you are and what you're called to accomplish as a precious gift. You can't live anyone else's life besides your own anyway, so you may as well get on with it and make the best of it. The best way to do this is to compare yourself to the best *you* that you can become. As John Newton said, "I am not what I ought to be. I am not what I want to be. I am not what I hope to be. But still, I am not what I used to be. And by the grace of God, I am what I am."

9. *You Will Be Frustrated by a Lack of Progress.*

There is a helpful saying that most people overestimate what they can accomplish in one year but underestimate what they can achieve in five. Most frustration is born of an unrealistic timeline expectation. Again, if you keep your eyes focused on your life's ziggurat, understanding that you are actualizing as much of your potential into your legacy as possible, you will be buffered against the frustration that usually comes from short-term thinking. The flip side of this, of course, is that you will be greatly encouraged when victories do come your way. The best strategy is to live off of the previous one until you can accomplish the next.

> **Most frustration is born of an unrealistic timeline expectation.**

10. *"They" Will Call You Lucky (or Say You Cheated).*

Albert Einstein said, "Great spirits have always encountered violent opposition from mediocre minds." There is something almost automatic about people wanting to take the shine off your achievements. Expect it. Of course, don't give them any ammunition for their weapons by living in such a way as to deserve such criticism, but rather drive them crazy with your glaring positive example of character and class. In the end, reputation is what people say about you, while character is what you really are. You are only in control of the second one of these; therefore, focus on it and let the dogs bark in the night. They are not yours to feed anyway.

The message is this: Success may be hard, but it's worth it, assuming, of course, that your definition of success is in line with the highest purpose you have set for yourself (or been called to) at the top of your ziggurat. Continue to pour out your potential into actualization by remembering that you are building your life into a masterpiece, and no difficulty encountered along the way can really stop you. Remember that problems are the seasoning that makes victory taste sweet.

> **Problems are the seasoning that makes victory taste sweet.**

– 4 –
Exertion

My two oldest sons, Casey and Nate, play competitive club soccer. It is accurate to say they are fanatics. My wife Terri and I have no idea where this came from, as neither of us knew much of anything about the sport prior to that first fateful trip to the local soccer facility years ago. It began as a bunch of four-year-olds clustering around a ball and has come home to roost as the single biggest terror by which our schedules have ever been assaulted. Every time we turn around (and we turn around a lot these days), there's another tournament, another out-of-state competition, or another camp or practice. When my boys are not playing soccer, they are watching it on satellite television, offering up perfect English accents in imitation of announcers and able to recite names of foreign players in five different countries.[1]

Instructively, however, they got to their individual playing levels by taking two very different paths. Casey, the oldest, was never the best player on any of his teams. He was always a decent participant but not dominant, especially in the early years. He always enjoyed it, however, and seemed to take it more seriously than many of the other kids on his teams.

Nate, on the other hand, having the advantage of three years of looking on and watching his older brother play, waiting impatiently in his pull-ups for his "big chance," practically exploded

---

[1] They are correcting me and telling me it's more than five, but in the words of Pontius Pilate, "I've written what I've written."

onto the scene. In almost every situation through the years, he's been his team's highest scorer and certainly one of the better players.[2] Today, both are pretty accomplished players enjoying themselves immensely and making contributions to top competitive teams. The point is that they got there in two entirely different ways.

Casey has worked hard consistently for over ten years. He is one of the most serious players at practice and works out and lifts weights to build his strength on his own time. He also is just as likely to ask me to take him to the nearby soccer fields to work on some part of his game as he is to sit down and relax. On the other hand, even though Nate has certainly worked hard too, much of his game has come from what his coaches say are the "unteachable" things. He just seems to be endowed with natural talent.

Multiple Routes to Success

The point of all this shameless bragging on my boys is to depict how the same result (in this case, being competitive soccer players) can come about in very different ways; there are multiple roads to accomplishment. This is helpful because we do not all begin from even starting positions. Everyone sets out from a unique beginning, with particular talents, abilities, and opportunities. These favor some and handicap others, depending upon the endeavor.

Perhaps you've felt a little behind other people in life. You didn't have the best upbringing, or you were held up or pushed down in some other way. No matter what you've tried to do, there has always been a little voice inside suggesting that you don't quite measure up to others, that you don't really have what it takes.

---

[2] Now before you get the idea that I'm one of those screaming dads who thinks his kids are phenoms and destined to rule the world with their game, I'm not. I am simply using them as an example. I am sure they are only slightly better than your kids.

Or to the contrary, maybe you've felt like you had a pretty good head start in life. You were given talents and opportunities that you've been able to rely upon for advancement to this point in your life. If you were honest with yourself, you would even admit that you've felt a little ahead of many people in your life. You know you've received gifts, and you enjoy using them.

People in both these scenarios need to understand a little more deeply the concept that there are multiple routes to success. Why? Because, over time, excellence becomes more and more about the effort the striver sustains and less and less about initial talent and advantageous beginnings.

The Formula for High Achievement

Most of us have a pretty good idea that high achievement is going to involve a heavy dose of hard effort. In fact, we've already discussed it. However, working hard is not the whole equation. It is quite possible to work extremely hard and never really get anywhere. This is because one can work hard but still not *smart*.

Working smart means doing things in the most advantageous way. Usually this involves learning from coaches and mentors or books and teachers who have more knowledge than you. The shortcut through a minefield is in the footsteps of someone who has already successfully made the crossing. While some trial and error is unavoidable and completely necessary along the way, the smartest work takes advantage of the knowledge of others. It has been said that experience is the best teacher, but in truth, other people's experience is the best.

So far in our formula for high achievement, we have *hard work* times *smart work*, and it is easy to see that these two are both a big part of achieving excellence in any field. However, there is a final factor to consider, without which nothing much happens.

That final factor is the powerful effect of *time*. It simply takes time to achieve expertise.

Katsushika Hokusai was a painter who lived in the late 1700s and early 1800s. According to Paul Johnson, "Hokusai, in effect, created Japanese landscape painting from nothing. Like Dürer... he was a combination of proper pride in his skills and modesty, fired by the determination to improve himself and do better."

In a letter to his publisher, Hokusai wrote:

> From the age of six I could draw forms and objects. By 50 I had turned out an infinite number of drawings. But I am not happy about anything I did before 70. Only at 73 did I begin to understand the true form of nature and birds, fish and plants. By 80 I had made a lot of progress. At 90 I will begin to get to the root of it all.

Earlier, we discussed the fact that people overestimate what they can accomplish in a short time but paradoxically seem to underestimate what they can achieve in a longer time. This is because almost everyone underestimates the power of compounding, which Einstein said (referring to interest on money) was the eighth wonder of the world.

Author Malcolm Gladwell has popularized research that indicates that about ten thousand hours of deliberate practice are required to attain mastery at any given task. The original research comes from, among others, neurologist Daniel Levitin, who wrote, "The emerging picture from such studies is that ten thousand hours of practice is required to achieve the level of mastery associated with being a world-class expert—in anything."

According to Gladwell, "No one has yet found a case in which true world-class expertise was accomplished in less time."

Researcher K. Anders Ericsson wrote in the paper entitled "The Role of Deliberate Practice in the Acquisition of Expert

Performance" that "deliberate practice makes all the difference. The differences between expert performers and normal adults reflect a life-long period of deliberate effort to improve performance in a specific domain."

We began this chapter with soccer, so let's consider an example from that sport. Sports statisticians Simon Kuper and Stefan Szymanski wrote:

> Why is it that so many of the best European soccer players—Zidane, Drogba, Ibrahimovic, Rooney, Cristiano Ronaldo—come from the poorest neighborhoods in Europe?...That reason is practice....In soccer, it is the poorest European boys who are most likely to reach the 10,000-hour mark....Their parents are less likely than middle-class parents to force them to waste precious time doing homework. And they have less money for other leisure pursuits. A constant in soccer players' ghosted autobiographies is the monomaniacal childhood spent playing nonstop soccer and, in a classic story, sleeping with a ball....By the time the boys were fifteen, they were much better players than suburban kids. The 10,000-hour rule also explains why blacks raised in American ghettos are overrepresented in basketball and football.

One should not look at all this research and merely think it takes a long time to become successful. That's missing the point. Instead, this information should be liberating because it proves that *anyone* can make it if he or she is willing to put in the requisite amount of time. And what's more,

> ***Anyone* can make it if he or she is willing to put in the requisite amount of time.**

most people *won't* do what it takes! That means there's relatively little competition "at the top." Geoff Colvin, a senior editor at *Fortune* magazine wrote, "The reality that deliberate practice is hard can even be seen as good news. It means that most people won't do it."

A research group from West Point, the University of Pennsylvania, and the University of Michigan conducted a study to determine why some students chose to continue pursuing military mastery while others fell off along the way. They found that the best predictor of success was something called "grit," which they defined as "perseverance and passion for long-term goals." They wrote, "Whereas the importance of working harder is easily apprehended, the importance of working longer without switching objectives may be less perceptible…in every field, grit may be as essential as talent to high accomplishment."

Therefore, the formula for high achievement looks like this:

Hard Work
×
Smart Work
×
10,000 Hours of Time (Grit)
=
World-Class Expertise

Victory to the "Try-Hards"

As even my boys in their early soccer experiences demonstrate, over time, hard and smart work can catch up to any advantages raw talent once provided. If Casey continues to work hard and put in productive practice with intentional personal growth, he can eventually outplay kids who previously outperformed him because of an early talent differential. On the other hand, if Nathaniel takes a lesson from this and multiplies the same formula of hard and smart work with the exponential power of time, he should be nearly unlimited in his potential. If he relies on his innate talent, however, he should expect to eventually be passed by those consistently trying harder.

These are the lessons from each of the scenarios we outlined above. Those who have always felt a little behind others and not quite worthy of the top honors can now realize that with enough hard work and enough smart work over time, anything is possible. To the contrary, those who have made it this far on talent and early advantages alone had better wake up to the truth that the "try-hards" are on the warpath and will overtake them if they don't plug into the same formula.

This is nothing new. Nearly a century ago, US President Calvin Coolidge uttered the famous advice:

> Nothing in this world can take the place of persistence. Talent will not; nothing is more common than unsuccessful people with talent. Genius will not; unrewarded genius is almost a proverb. Education will not; the world is full of educated derelicts. Persistence and determination alone are omnipotent. The slogan 'press on' has solved and always will solve the problems of the human race.

This, of course, rings true as long as that "pressing on" is done in a smart way, as we have seen.

The Exponential Power of Exertion

Why should all this be so? Why, exactly, does hard work times smart work over enough time lead to expertise? Author Jeff Olson called it "the slight edge." His book so entitled explains how that little bit of extra effort, over time, works to separate the achiever from the rest of the pack. It wasn't until I drew out a graph that I truly understood the means behind his claims. Maybe it is the engineer in me, but I couldn't help it. Here is the graph:

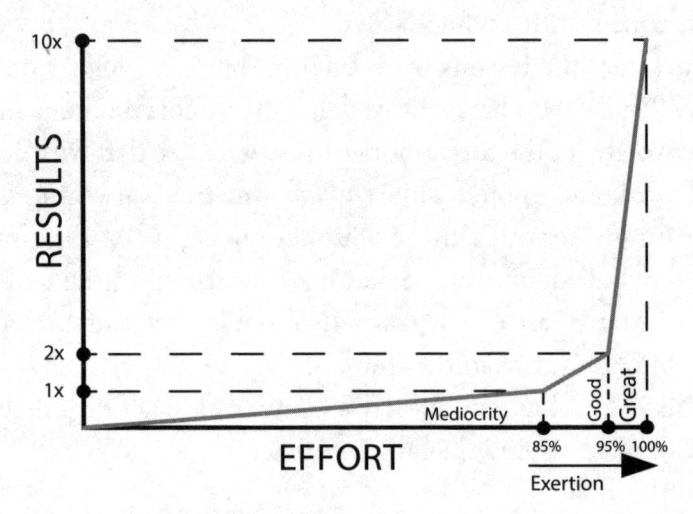

In this approximated graph, we can see that a vast majority of the people are pretty much living in mediocrity. They are putting in average effort and largely getting the same mediocre results. In fact, it can be proven that most people are average. Humorously, however, most people think they are actually *above* average. Mathematically this cannot be true, but there is something hardwired in our nature, apparently, to overestimate our position in life relative to others.

Cornell researchers David Dunning and Justin Kruger actually published a finding about this very phenomenon that was so insightful that it won the satirical "Ig Nobel Prize" in psychology for the year 2000. Ultimately, Dunning and Kruger determined that people have a cognitive bias in which unskilled individuals suffer from "illusory superiority" that is responsible for them mistakenly rating their ability higher than average. In other words, people tend to think they're "all that and a bag of chips" when, more realistically, they're just the bag of chips.

> **People tend to think they're "all that and a bag of chips" when, more realistically, they're just the bag of chips.**

Incidentally, this is why certain people shy away from competition—because they dislike being measured objectively. They are more comfortable in their own self-deception than being confronted with the reality of their performance (or lack thereof). People in true pursuit of excellence, however, do not allow themselves this luxury of hiding from the scoreboard. They face up to the glaring spotlight of objectivity and use the data to improve themselves.

Back to the graph.

The rare individuals who dare to exert more effort than average will, over time, accomplish higher results. Because, as the workload increases, there are fewer and fewer people willing to subject themselves to such intensity, the curve becomes exponential. In other words, the curve turns up steeply because there are far fewer people fighting for those results. Another reason for the sharp upward curve is that peak effort maximizes much more quickly than lower numbers. In financial terms, it's the rich getting richer because, though the multiplier is the same, the amount of capital is much larger.

Actualization

Tony Hsieh, CEO of Zappos.com Inc., wrote the following in a letter to his organization:

> It's hard...but if we weren't doing something hard, then we'd have no business. The only reason we aren't swamped by our competition is because what we do is hard, and we do it better than anyone else. If it ever gets too easy, then start looking for a tidal wave of competition to wash us away.
>
> It may seem sometimes like we don't know what we're doing. And it's true: we don't...but you can take comfort in knowing that nobody else knows how to do what we're doing either.

Note that if one exerts just 10 percent more effort than most of the rest, the results nearly double. But if one adds merely another few percent beyond that, the results are as much as ten times more! This is what author Jeff Olson was teaching in so many words. For those who will exert themselves just that slight amount more, over time, there will be little to no competition. The results will be astoundingly greater.

> **For those who will exert themselves just that slight amount more, over time, there will be little to no competition.**

Wide receiver Jerry Rice was not the biggest, nor the fastest, nor as talented as many other men the same age who played the same position. Nonetheless, he is often talked about as the best in the history of the National Football League and sometimes even considered to be the best all-around football player ever. Yet in his youth, he was only able to garner a collegiate scholarship from the relatively small and unknown school Mississippi Valley State. His professional prospects were quite a bit better, based upon his collegiate performance, but still, experts didn't expect him to be picked up until the sixth or seventh round in the NFL draft.

One coach, however, understood his worth. Bill Walsh of the San Francisco Forty-Niners was looking for exactly the kind of player Rice had made himself into—quick, precise, and incredibly hard-working. With this basic foundation, Walsh knew he had found what he was looking for to complete his high-percentage offense featuring the accurate and consistent quarterback, Joe Montana. For the next twenty years, Jerry Rice continued to work at an intimidating pace to perfect his craft. Even after winning multiple Super Bowls and MVP awards, Rice demonstrated an uncommon hunger to push himself to maximum effort in the pursuit of excellence.

A man who began with perhaps only above-average talent, with literally hundreds of others "ahead" of him on the talent scale, had worked himself into icon status. How did he do it? Rice exerted himself consistently and smartly over time. His workouts and practice sessions were legendary in the league. Often young hotshot players would join Rice in his training, certain they could show up "the old guy." Rice almost always left them in the dust with their tongues hanging out. That's how intense he was. Colvin wrote, "The records he holds for total receptions, total touchdown receptions, and total receiving yards are greater than the second-place totals not by 5 percent or 10 percent, which would be impressive, but by about 50 percent." By consistently outworking everyone in his position, Rice eventually outperformed them as well.

The next logical question, though, is this: How do you go about revving yourself up high enough to put in this kind of effort over time? Of course, for part of the answer, we must go back to the ziggurat construct. For those who are in line with their passions and calling, aiming upward, as it were, to those lofty aspirations, the "work" won't seem as much like work, and all this will be more bearable. For the other half of the answer, we must turn to the next chapter.

– 5 –
Immersion

In the original version of the movie *The Karate Kid*, Mr. Miyagi famously exhorted young Daniel-san to "paint the fence," then "sand the floor," and then "wax the car." After these apparently pointless exercises went on too long for young Daniel's attention span, the wise Mr. Miyagi (also known for catching flies with chopsticks) quickly demonstrated that all those hours of rote training in basic hand motions had in fact imparted some fundamentals. Miyagi simply needed to yell out the appropriate chore motion, such as "wax on," and Daniel, to his astonishment, would circle his hand in an effective blocking motion. To this day, if I attempt to wrestle or slap-box with my brother Pat, he will begin defending himself and simultaneously call out, "Wax on," "Wax off," and "Sand the floor."

Three Stages to Mastery

There are three stages in life on the road to mastery of any craft.

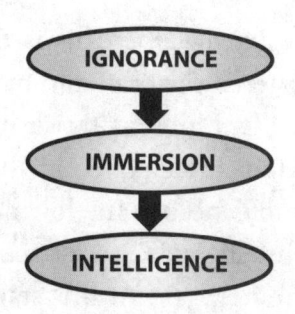

IGNORANCE
↓
IMMERSION
↓
INTELLIGENCE

The first is called *Ignorance*. This is the brief but enjoyable stage in which the task at hand seems interesting and enjoyable. Without the confusion of knowledge, accidental competence sometimes occurs, and practitioners are often able to make some early headway quite easily. At this early stage, it is easy to take things too lightly, underestimate the top performers in the category, and even get a little cocky. In the case of young Daniel-san, he didn't even know what he didn't know. He was being initiated into the basics of karate without even realizing it.

The next stage is called *Immersion*. This stage is the key. As we saw in the previous chapter, without long-term immersion in a topic, mastery will never be realized. This takes intensity, focus, commitment, and time. The challenge here is that as one plunges into the craft, all sorts of details and complexity that weren't apparent before begin to reveal themselves. Things begin to seem overwhelming and difficult. What at first looked fun and easy soon begins to feel impossible and perhaps no longer worth it. There is a clear choice to be made in the immersion stage: Feel the pressure or marvel at the wonder. It is possible to do both productively, but never just the first. A healthy sense of wonder at all that is involved is required for ongoing enthusiasm and commitment long term.

> There is a clear choice to be made in the immersion stage: Feel the pressure or marvel at the wonder.

The final stage is *Intelligence*. This is the stage in which the practitioner has mastered the craft and makes it look easy to the outside world. Outsiders look at those with such mastery and say they have a certain intelligence in the topic, as in "Peyton Manning has incredible football intelligence." We now know that if Peyton has such intelligence, it is strictly a direct result of his years of hard and smart work. At this stage, competence is now second nature and almost unconscious, although the job of the master to continually improve never ends.

A Punch Is Just a Punch

Sticking with the theme of *The Karate Kid*, we can consider these three steps from the standpoint of martial arts. Let's consider the incredible example that something as seemingly rudimentary as a punch provides.

Upon first look, it may appear that throwing a punch is nothing more than that—simply throwing a punch. However, once immersion in martial arts begins, the student realizes that there are complex and specific mechanics involved in properly throwing a punch, such as body position, center of gravity, core involvement, opposing hand pullback, torso twist, formation of the fist, pointing of lead knuckles, and much more.

It is in this stage that one realizes that a punch is *more* than just a punch. After thousands and thousands of practice punches in a host of different environments and applications, honed to sharpness by the oversight of a master sensei (perhaps a Mr. Miyagi) over a long time, eventually a punch returns to being "just a punch"—meaning it becomes second nature and almost automatic. However, now it is extremely effective and correctly done.

The Pressure of the Process

One of the biggest challenges with the immersion stage is the pressure of the process that results. The desire to achieve excellence and the push and the drive required to sustain hard work and practice over the long haul combine to put pressure on the participant. Unfortunately, many people do not handle this well. Unaccustomed to pressure as a productive resource, they react incorrectly to it and:

1. Become overwhelmed, determine that the task is too hard, and quit.
2. Cave in to the pressure but don't quit, yet also don't bring the concentration and effort required to pass through the immersion stage to mastery. Instead, they wallow around in immersion indefinitely, going through the motions halfheartedly and never really improving. Orrin Woodward relates this principle to people who claim to have thirty years of work experience, when actually in many cases, they merely have one year of experience thirty times over.
3. Blame the craft or the process. This is precisely where Daniel-san found himself. This often turns people into "suggestion machines," as in "This craft would be so much better if they would just make such and such changes...." Unwittingly, the productive pressure of the immersion stage is bled off and applied elsewhere, in essence, externally. Relieving this pressure by directing it outward instead of inward robs the participant of the lessons the pressure brings and prolongs the time required to reach mastery.
4. Blame other people for their own lack of progress. This is even worse than blaming the task itself because now it also involves playing the part of a victim. This is a total relief of the productive pressure and is the surest way to become entrapped in the immersion stage long term or even to take the short trip back to #1 above and quit outright.

These four reactions are bad enough in themselves because they are progress killers. But they are also sad because they deprive the individual of the productive power that pressure provides. We've all heard that a diamond is simply a piece of coal that was subjected to intense pressure for a long, long time. Pressure, properly utilized, can be an enormously productive thing. And this is especially true for someone pursuing excellence.

Champions know that it's the pressure that makes them great. They learn not to run from this pressure, become discouraged by it, or quit but instead to channel it into greater intensity and focus. As soccer great Steve Bull said of the butterflies in his stomach before a big game, "Nerves and butterflies are fine—they're a physical sign that you're mentally ready and eager. You have to get the butterflies to fly in formation; that's the trick." Bull had it right: We need to channel the pressure and make it work *for* us, not against us. The key to staying in the immersion phase, the key to exertion as we discussed in the last chapter, is to properly handle the pressure that is natural to the process. You do this by transforming it into intensity and then by focusing that intensity on your improvement.

Focus

Time spread too thinly across too many activities is another killer for anyone truly seeking mastery. There simply isn't enough time to become a master at more than a few things in life. Time doesn't wait. Health doesn't last. Windows of opportunity don't remain open. Relationships will not wait forever. Time lost is time lost. Period. As discussed in the previous chapter, mastery is only available if given enough time, and either delaying or restarting immersion or else spreading oneself too thin can deprive one of the time required.

Also, one can easily observe that attempting to compete part-time with someone dedicated full-time to a profession is likely an exercise in futility. Sooner or later, the per-

> **Sooner or later, the person with the most focus, the most commitment, the most "skin in the game," will win.**

son with the most focus, the most commitment, the most "skin in the game," will win.

In order to take the fullest advantage of life immersed in a worthy pursuit, one must focus. We are all busy. There are many, many different responsibilities in life. We have family obligations, work responsibilities, friendships, and other interests. However, mastery requires concentrated immersion in the subject at hand. The more concentrated our focus, the more quickly proficiency and expertise will result. This should be obvious, but for immersion to work, we must be *immersed*. That means throwing ourselves all the way in. There is no partial immersion. Immersion works because, like the hokey pokey, it requires us to throw our whole selves in.

Personal Management

We still have not fully answered the question how one can maintain sufficient intensity to stay in the immersion stage for the long haul. In the last chapter, we reflected back that one part of the answer involves properly reading our ziggurat diagram to make sure all the effort is aimed toward building the correct monument, meaning our hard work is in line with our highest aspirations of purpose while also taking advantage of our passions. So far, so good. But what else must be done? As we have just seen, there are dangers of quitting and distraction to be avoided. Ultimately, though, staying in the immersion stage long term is a product of the level of our *personal management*.

John Wooden, record-setting coach of the UCLA basketball team and one of the most successful coaches in any sport, wrote:

> Activity—to produce real results—must be organized and executed meticulously. Otherwise, it's no different from children running around the playground at recess. Time, used correctly, is among your most potent as-

sets. For many leaders, however, it seems otherwise. The months, weeks, and minutes are ill-defined and almost intangible in their minds, evaporating without leaving a trace of achievement behind. In the mind of those leaders whose organizations get things done, time is tangible, a commodity as touchable as gold. The success of my leadership was directly linked to using time wisely. Respect time, and it will respect you.

This is personal management of the highest magnitude. Note that any consideration of personal management necessarily involves a focus on what you are doing with your time. (Gandalf, anyone?) But it also involves other aspects, such as how you think, the management of your attitude, and your overall hunger to accomplish your purpose.

There are a few practical things to seek out in order to maintain the highest level of personal management and thereby keep yourself fully locked into the immersion stage.

1. **Informational Reinforcement:** To stay sharp and continue learning and growing, one needs to be plugged into a source of information about the craft at hand. Read all you can about your pursuit. Listen to audio recordings as well. Peruse trade magazines, and familiarize yourself with any and all websites of authority pertaining to your field. Find out if there are events or symposiums, concerts or competitions that you can attend and use as educational experiences. Gathering and digesting all the information you can get your hands on for your particular area of chosen mastery will keep you fresh and be a shortcut forward in your development.
2. **Relational Reinforcement:** There is an old joke that goes like this: "Two idiots and one genius go into a room to-

gether. After a time, out come three idiots." Beyond being funny, it clearly illustrates the power of association with others. Choose your associations wisely (as the wrong ones can be incredibly wrong). Make sure you are hanging around with people who are experts in the endeavor you are pursuing. Find yourself a Mr. Miyagi and wash the heck out of his car, sand his floors until they shine, and paint his fence like Tom Sawyer's friends. The reinforcement you get from mentors and experts in your field will quiet the voices of dissent around you who don't understand what you're doing or why.

3. **Self-Talk:** In one of the odder techniques available, many of the top masters in their fields long ago had to learn to stop listening to themselves and instead begin talking to themselves. This is because our minds are quickly capable of "going negative" on us, and, believe it or not, our own words to ourselves are very powerful. For this reason, practice the art of positive self-talk. This can be done through affirmation statements and memorized phrases of encouragement (Bible verses are also good for this) to keep yourself focused and provide a quick recentering when your wheels begin to wobble.

The Immersion Engine

In my early years as an engineer, I became fascinated by Mazda's rotary engine. The only major auto manufacturer with a rotary engine on the market, Mazda was something of an enigma to me. Why would a car company build production motors so entirely different and so distinct from the standard piston engines made by everyone else? To attempt to answer this question, I read articles, analyzed diagrams, and eventually test-drove one of the cars myself. Indeed, there was a notable smoothness to the engine. And it was very quiet. These attributes were nice, but I never really got myself to understand why they would stick with such a different strategy.

Years later though, when I came across all the research about deliberate practice and the concepts of mastery, I immediately thought back to Mazda's rotary engine. You see: A rotary engine is composed of lobes, roughly shaped like triangles, attached along the length of a shaft. This assembly then turns inside a cylinder. As the corners of the lobes make their way around inside the shaft, the compression of the air-fuel mixture can be ignited by a spark plug and the resulting explosion serves to push on the lobe, thereby turning the shaft and generating power output. To get the whole thing going requires an electric motor to turn the assembly and a spark from a spark plug, just as with a piston engine. But once the shaft is spinning and the compressed gases are being combusted, the shaft spins nicely, devoid of all the opposing up-and-down motions of piston engines. This is why rotary engines are so much smoother.

What does all this have to do with immersion and the concepts of attaining mastery in a particular area? We have been discussing hard work and smart work and the power of these things to produce expertise over time. The diagram below shows the *way* this works, and it just happens to look a lot like a rotary engine!

From this, we can see that one thing leads to and actually *fuels* the next. With proper practice, normally an improvement in results is seen, and this, in turn, inspires the participant to greater passion for the subject at hand. We are all encouraged by progress. This fuels the passion to practice more and even more intensely, which leads to greater results, which fuels more passion…and on and on the little rotary engine of immersion goes.

There are a few things to note about this process. First, an external spark is required to initiate the whole thing. This might be a push or early exposure to the topic from parents, a challenge from a coworker, or an external ambition such as obtaining a degree or hitting a particular business goal. It is always some external stimulus that starts the cycle in motion.

Next, practice must be specific and targeted to develop improvement. It's not enough to merely "put in the time"; one must instead practice *deliberately*. This involves focusing in on key areas that align with one's gifts and talents. It requires specificity and should be guided by an expert who knows how best to focus your efforts. This is why mentors and coaches are so important.

> It's not enough to merely "put in the time"; one must instead practice *deliberately*.

Practice leads to results. These results must be monitored and evaluated. As the old saying goes, "You can only expect what you are willing to inspect." Measurement is critical, as it provides an objective scoreboard on one's progress and also gives direction for changes in the practice for future improvement.

Increased results provide encouragement. This fuels the passion to work even harder. Passion, however, must also be stimulated and supported. This means that the environment where all this is taking place should be soaked with positive reinforcement. Like engine oil that reduces friction and carries away destructive heat buildup, the reinforcements of information, relationships, and self-talk discussed above are applied here.

At the center of the engine, the crankshaft, so to speak, is your intrinsic motivation. This is the heart of it all. This represents your hunger for excellence, your desire to attain expertise, and your overall inner drive to fulfill your life's great purpose. It might be clear now why we began the book with these deepest of considerations (the top of the ziggurat) because the internal drives are critical to keeping this little engine of immersion running. Ultimately, excellence and expertise have to be an inside job. Long term, no one can push you to do these things; you've got to push yourself.

Understand: You alone have to decide to master your craft. Someone else may have gotten you started, but in time, you must fall in love with the wonder of the depth of what you do. This is the beauty of the immersion phase: It will fuel your intensity and magnify your focus. Excellence will require that you throw your whole self into the endeavor and become a patient student of the process, using the pressure wisely and allowing it to mold you over time into a legitimate master, one with that special "intelligence" in your field.

– 6 –

Some

During medieval and Renaissance times in Florence, Italy, there existed little deposit boxes all around the city called *tamburi*, which were named after the small musical drums which they resembled. Another name for them was *buchi della verità*, meaning "holes of truth." The purpose of these receptacles was to receive denunciations against Florence's citizens. The accusations themselves, little slips of paper written by anonymous accusers, were called *tamburazioni*. Leading figures including Leonardo da Vinci and Niccolò Machiavelli were accused of all manner of horrendous behavior and crimes via these cowardly devices. And such accusations were not taken lightly. An enforcement body called "The Lords of Eight" was often vicious in its prosecution of the accused.

Why People Quit Something Worthy

We can be thankful that criticism in our day is not quite as systematized or legally damning as the *tamburazioni* of early Florence. Nevertheless, critics and their negativity still have immense power to rob us of our joy and to pull us off the path toward excellence and achievement. Cowards, critics, cynics, detractors, naysayers, and slanderers, even without organized *tamburi* around your town, will still be on hand to squawk at your greatest efforts. With the advent of the Internet, anyone and everyone has a voice. While this is good and bad, critics have found that online, they get the same type of anonymity as the Florentine *tamburi* but with no legal follow-up. They can say anything they want, whether it is substantiated or not, and they usually do.

We must remember that critics are merely spectators. They have no power to stop us beyond what we ourselves give them. It is also helpful to realize that nothing of significance was ever achieved without negative input from other people. All those who lived great lives before you had to learn this fact. They dealt with it, and so can you. A good mental framework is the reminder that if the wrong people are not criticizing you, then you may not be doing the right things!

> **Nothing of significance was ever achieved without negative input from other people.**

The negative input of others is just one of the reasons people are tempted to quit something worthy. In fact, there are many more. In considering each of these, we can be aware of the dangers that lurk along our path to greatness and take evasive action.

One of the predominant reasons people quit something worthy is pride. It is hard on some people's self-image to play the part of the amateur, to make mistakes, and to appear foolish by being new at something. I am reminded of a newborn colt trying to stand for the first time. It wobbles unsteadily and attempts to rise atop spindly legs, looking nearly ridiculous in the process. Practitioners new to any craft must appear the same way. It is a hard, cold truth that to become good at something requires being bad at it first. All of us have to go through being awkward before we can be smooth. If there is something worth doing, it's worth doing poorly long enough to learn to do it

> **If there is something worth doing, it's worth doing poorly long enough to learn to do it well.**

well. Many people cannot handle this initial awkwardness and therefore shy away from the attempt, or else they quit once it's obvious they might look foolish. Sadly, in such cases, looking successful is apparently more important than actually becoming successful.

Another factor that leads to quitting is a lack of character. This can take many forms, such as addictions or besetting sins that are destructive in a person's life. Obviously, these are extreme examples, but they are real to a surprisingly large number of people. Other failures of character are dishonesty, lack of integrity, and overall untrustworthiness. People with failures of character cannot make it long term because they get found out. Then, once their failures are discovered, they are forced to quit and take their act elsewhere. It's similar to the man who was changing his son's diaper and accidentally got some of the stinky stuff on his finger. Throughout the day, everywhere he went, he smelled something foul. To him, every room in the house stank. But the problem wasn't with each of the different rooms in his house; the problem was with *him*. People lacking character live this scenario out in actual life. Until the root character issues are dealt with squarely, they will be forced to quit time and again to hide their shortcomings—because everywhere they go, there they are.[1]

Perhaps surprisingly, comfort is another reason people quit the pursuit of something challenging. In effect, they give in to the lure of lesser things. This is mainly a failure of short-term considerations taking precedence over long-term ones. In these instances, people are surrendering what they deeply want in the long run for what they sort of want in the moment. Author Robert Greene wrote, "Too many people believe that everything must be pleasurable in life, which makes them constantly search for distractions." The antidote for this is to keep your eyes

---

1 Stinking up the joint.

Actualization

on where you're heading. Remember your ziggurat. Don't be tempted to trade in the long-term *great* for a short-term *good*. Remember that you are building a monument out of your life, and in order for it to be all it should be, much of the journey won't be comfortable.

Another reason people quit something worthy is the lack of a large enough dream. "It wasn't worth it anyway," someone might say in this instance. This is a clear indication that their original motivation wasn't strong enough. They, in effect, didn't have a big enough reason *why*. I am not the biggest fan of nineteenth-century philosopher Friedrich Nietzsche. (For one thing, he had a most horrendous moustache.) But there is one quote in particular that is attributed to him that I like: "He who has a Why to live for can bear almost any How." This is true to the extreme. Staying in touch with our motivations, our dreams, our desires, and yes, our passions and callings as shown by our ziggurat model is the key to perseverance long term. What most people don't realize is that motivation is their own responsibility. In the long run, the drive for excellence and mastery must be intentionally cultivated like a good garden. In order to accomplish the God-given desires of one's heart, a person must continually foster his or her hunger to do so.

> **In the long run, the drive for excellence and mastery must be intentionally cultivated like a good garden.**

Relational challenges are another catalyst for quitting. As stated above, almost all success depends upon successfully working with other people. Selfishness, combativeness, rudeness, harshness, irritability, a mean spirit, and a long list of additional vices can fray or tear the fabric of key relationships. Hurt feelings and a lack of drive are the result. Being relational beings, we humans nearly stop functioning when our relationships have gone awry. My friend Dr. Doug Bookman once observed, "the most soul-numbing sense of despair you have ever known or *could* ever know…was not ultimately or substantively about finances, or about health, or about politics. It had to do with *relationships*." Such a pain, if associated with our pursuits, will make us feel like giving them up. To stay away from this paralyzing feeling of futility, we must do all we can to build strong personal bonds with others—to attract and maintain good friendships and become a good friend, to get help from others and be a big help to them. This category is important enough to warrant extra study. Read the good books on personal relationships and apply what you learn to always continue growing in this area. It will be very important in the long run.

There are many other reasons people quit worthy endeavors, including an unwillingness to accept personal responsibility, self doubt, and a lack of mental toughness. In fact, we could probably continue for pages and pages expounding more and more such reasons. But this list is sufficient. The key point to remember is that there are many exit ramps along the road to success, and most of them will be tempting.

Ramifications of Quitting

We have spent so much time on the topic of quitting because it is particularly wasteful. This is due to the fact that it mercilessly starts the process of immersion over from scratch. Quitters often enjoy immediate relief from the pressure or tedium of immersion and even brag about it to others. But masters know that this temporary respite from pressure is simply the pause in the timeline until the person must choose the next endeavor and begin the process all over again. Sadly, the cycle usually just repeats itself as the person gets frustrated with the next new pursuit and quits again.

It is precisely in this fashion, blaming processes and people all along the way, that many would-be achievers accomplish very little with their lives and never actually master anything. Time ticks by without remorse as self-deceived people entrap themselves in unnecessary mediocrity, spilling much of their potential instead of depositing it into their legacy.

> **Quitting is a permanent solution to a temporary problem.**

There is nothing wrong with the impulse to quit. In fact, you will be tempted to quit every good thing you ever do in your life. The problem is that quitting is a permanent solution to a temporary problem.

Believe it or not, most problems have a way of working out over time. Problems are a lot like weeds. They may be unsightly. They may be annoying. But they are rarely fatal. Quitting is like giving away a valuable piece of lakefront property simply because weeds grew on it. There are much less extreme ways to rid the lot of its weeds than getting rid of it entirely.

Perhaps the worst thing about quitting is that it begins a habit in your life. The short-term high resulting from the pressure relief can be addicting. Go for it often enough, and you'll never stay in the immersion stage long enough to accomplish anything worthwhile, much less reach mastery in a subject.

Finally, quitting sets a terrible example for others. No matter who you are, it is very likely that you are an influencer upon someone, if not several someones. Don't let them down by wimping out partway into something worthy. Give them a good example by hanging tough. Remember that if what you're fighting for matters, the obstacles don't.

It's for Whom It's For

A final consideration for keeping yourself sharp and in the immersion stage is to realize that, as we've already stated, your greatest output will not be loved and admired by everyone. Consequently, you will need a mental process to run in your head when you are hit with direct criticism for what you do. Here is one that might help. I came to it quite by accident.

One of my recent books (never mind which) had just come out on the market and seemed to be well received by readers. I happened to glance at a list of reader comments and their corresponding ratings, ranging from five (or "great") to one ("terrible"). For the most part, the book was receiving fives (thanks, Mom)! In fact, very few ratings weren't a five; there were a small number of fours and perhaps one three, and that was about it.

Then I spotted something I couldn't believe. One lady (bless her heart) had rated the book a *one*. I know! I was shocked, too! But there it was for all the world to see. Curiosity got the best of me, and I quickly read her full commentary. It was obvious immediately that she hadn't understood my humor and had taken some of the things I'd written entirely out of context. In effect, she just didn't "get it."

I must admit that for some reason, this one lady's disapproval nearly outweighed all the many fine praises others were giving the book. One lady! There was just something depressing about realizing that not *everyone* loved my book. I mean, come on! I had worked hard on that thing. I had sweat blood at the keyboard, argued with editors, and nurtured each of those sentences into print with the care of a doting father. To be stabbed through the back with the sharp dagger of a rating of *one* was just too much.

Then I did something smart (accidentally, of course). I noticed that the website had provided a handy histogram, or bar chart, summarizing the reader scores. Sure enough, it showed almost all fives, a chunk of fours, a lone three, and that single lowly one down there at the bottom. This chart gave a quick visual summary of reader opinion in one quick glance. This (and here comes the smart part) allowed me to click through books written by other authors to see what readers thought of *their* work. Of course, I began with my favorite books. I clicked on Patrick O'Brian, in my mind, one of English prose's great masters. Shockingly, there were people who *hated* his books! I clicked on Herman Wouk and his most famous and very successful books. Same thing. Then I clicked through most of the timeless classics and then on to some of today's most popular literature. I was discovering that the relatives of that lady were everywhere! All these great authors were getting the same kind of results: lots of fives, a lesser number of fours, even fewer threes, then usually more twos, and even more ones. In fact, their overall charts usually looked like this:[2]

For these books, there was always a population of readers who *loved* them or *hated* them, with very few people in between.

But wait. There's more.

Next, I clicked through random books and books I didn't particularly like. Interestingly, *most* of these books showed a *different* pattern from the one just described. In most cases, there were few fives, more fours, the most threes, followed by fewer twos, and finally only a few ones. Their charts looked like this, the very opposite of the other chart:

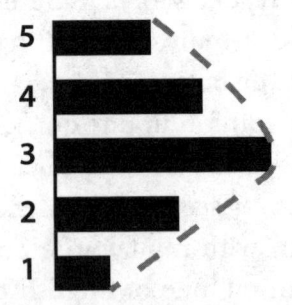

---

[2] Mine, too, with time on the market, would eventually get more and more ones, rounding out to look more like this same shape.

From this, I discovered that, according to readers, there were really only three kinds of books out there: books they loved, books they hated, and books that left them lukewarm. This was a revelation. It seemed that, at least according to the readers on this particular website, if someone was going to love a book, that automatically meant others would hate it. However, if very few people *loved* a book, very few would *hate* it either. On such books, most readers were somewhere in the middle.

This was an epiphany to me! I realized that greatness polarizes. It attracts rabid fans on one side and just-as-rabid anti-fans on the other. I thought of the vitriol poured out on George W. Bush during his years as president and then the fanatical negativity aimed at Barack Obama. Yet both these men were able to garner tens of millions of votes to sit in the highest office in the land! There were people who loved them *and* people who hated them. I thought of those who love Tom Cruise as an actor and those who can't stand him. And of course, I thought of those of us who (quite rightfully) hate the Pittsburgh Steelers and those pitiful souls who follow them fanatically. Example after example scurried through my mind like the escaping kids in *Chitty Chitty Bang Bang*.

> **Greatness polarizes.**

Now, I am not saying this means my book was great—simply that I took comfort in the fact that other books had this same tendency to polarize. I also was encouraged that mine left almost no one lukewarm. Immediately, I looked up the Bible verse I remembered saying something about this lukewarm stuff. I found it in Revelation 3:16 (NASB): "So because you are lukewarm, and neither hot nor cold, I will spit you out of My mouth." Okay, so God was talking about a particular church in Asia Minor at the time, but still, it's pretty obvious from that verse that lukewarm is not a desirable thing.

Actualization

Here's the point: When you are pursuing your purposeful calling and aligning your passions toward that end, attempting to master your craft and achieve excellence, all that is no guarantee that some people still won't "get it."

> There will *always* be people who don't get it.

There will *always* be people who don't get it. Take that to heart, and what's more, don't worry about those whom what you do is *not* for; instead, focus only upon those whom it *is* for!

We seem to carry our rejections too heavily and our encouragements too lightly, when actually, they go together to form a complete picture. It's not dislike that should discourage us but rather *indifference*. What's most demoralizing is when people really don't care about what you do one way or the other. So don't worry if you get people who hate what you do. That's okay. And be doubly sure not to change what you do in an effort to please *them*.

> Don't *conform* for critics; *perform* for fans.

You'll *never* please that crowd! You are not *for* them! If you focus any energy trying to please those you're *not* for, you will change how you do things and simultaneously stop thrilling those you *are* for![3] In other words, don't *conform* for critics; *perform* for fans.

I am reminded of the Sawyer Brown song entitled "Some Girls Do." The lyrics are especially good to remember if you're a single young man being rejected by a young lady. "Well, I ain't first class, but I ain't white trash. I'm wild and a little crazy, too. Some girls don't like boys like me. Aw, but some girls do!" But the concept applies to anything worth pursuing. Not everyone will like what you do or who you are. But *some* will. It's for those *some* that you give it all you've got and never stop.

---

3 Have you ever seen so many prepositions at the ends of sentences? It's something I didn't plan on. I just felt I had to. It's something I never thought of.

Legacy (and Spillage)

POTENTIAL

ACTUALIZATION

LEGACY   SPILLAGE

What Will It Matter?

– 7 –

Meaning

In 280 BC, Tarentum was a Greek colony on the southern tip of the Italian peninsula located inside the "heel of the boot." One of the cities of the Greek colonial territory then known as Magna Graecia, Tarentum found itself at odds with the growing might of the Romans, its neighbors to the north. War broke out, and King Pyrrhus of Epirus was called upon to honor his agreement with the people of Tarentum to return the support his kingdom had earlier received from them against his own enemies. Pyrrhus was eager for glory and didn't hesitate to sail with an army to their aid. What followed were several very costly victories, in which Pyrrhus's armies defeated the Roman, Samnite, Etruscan, and Thurii adversaries (such is the complexity of ancient battles).

After one such engagement in which Pyrrhus lost approximately 4,000 men, and upon being congratulated for yet another victory, the king said something along the lines of "Another victory like this, and I'm done for!" We know of him today mostly because of the term *Pyrrhic victory* used in modern parlance, which was taken from this saying and refers to victories won at too high a cost. Historian Anthony Everitt wrote, "Pyrrhus achieved almost nothing that lasted. For all the brilliance, energy, and charm, a cloud of pointlessness hangs over Pyrrhus's career." Yes, but at *least* he has a famous term based on his name.

Millions of other humans have been remembered (or forgotten) for even less.

One Saturday morning in my adolescence, I happened upon my father in the garage. He was cleaning out some old toolboxes and suddenly handed me a hammer. It was as common as any hammer could be, with the exception of a name handprinted boldly down the length of its wooden handle in permanent black ink: *Andrew Jackson Brady*. "That belonged to my grandfather," said my dad, "your great-grandfather." He went on to explain that this was pretty much our only family heirloom, and it was to be mounted in a special display box. Being young and therefore on my way out to do something as important as nothing in particular, I didn't think much about it at the time. But years later when I inquired about this hammer, I learned that the shop to which it had been taken for mounting had long since been forgotten and the hammer, our only ancestral artifact, had tragically disappeared. By then, I was old enough to appreciate it and bemoaned the fact of its loss, but to no avail. Andrew Jackson Brady had written his name on that hammer in vain.

Almost.

I got to thinking about old Andrew Jackson Brady one day and realized that we know more about him than we do almost *any* of our other ancestors. In fact, summing up his life's work, it's twice as memorable as nearly all the others. Consider this: Most of those names that appear in genealogical records give us pretty much only one piece of information about each person: whom they fathered or mothered. In other words, we know only one thing that they did in their lives.

Come back to Andrew Jackson Brady, and you'll immediately see that, not only do we know *that* about him, but in his illustrious life, he also did something else: to wit, he wrote his name on a tool! Now I ask you, do you think he realized that he was about to perform the second most memorable act of his life when he

MEANING

uncapped that marker those many years ago? If you think these considerations a little fanciful, can you think of more than basic information about the lives of most of your ancestors? Do you even know their names?

My wife has an uncle who is a wonder at researching genealogy. Occasionally, he sends us articles and CD-ROMs loaded with information. I will confess that families fortunate enough to have such an uncle retain much more information about the lives of ancestors than usual. However, even with the exhaustive abilities of Uncle Charles, one article in particular caught my eye. It pertained to a certain man in my wife's family tree who was reported in the local agricultural paper as having driven his buckboard wagon into town one day to purchase a bushel of oats. That's all history knows about him. There. Another example. I doubt it's possible this man had any inkling in his mind as he rattled the rutty roads into town that he was about to perform the second most memorable act of his entire existence, even something that would be written about in a book a century and a half later!

It boggles the mind.

The point to take from all this certainly isn't that doing something memorable is the same as doing something meaningful or important. Certainly lasting fame or remembrance is not a true measure of greatness and excellence, nor is it worthy of a direct aim with one's life as though it were a purposeful calling. If doing something memorable were the key, we should all go to our toolboxes immediately to write our names upon everything. Still, it makes you think, doesn't it? We live, we love, we lose, we struggle, we strive, we die, and within a couple generations, the only thing left is people who know nothing of us but may, perhaps, have our nose or our eyes. I wouldn't mind if they also had my hammer, to be honest.

Legacy (and Spillage)

Kurt Cobain was born less than a month before I was, I remember thinking in 1991. It was the year in which he and his band Nirvana exploded onto the popular music scene with their second album entitled *Nevermind*. Cobain and company had created a new, edgy sound, with incredibly harsh guitar and vocals to match.[1] They would be credited as the official initiators and leading band of what came to be called "grunge," which would transform popular music in ways that can still be heard today. Cobain and his band's accomplishments are nothing short of spectacular. Beyond their creative and artistic acclaim, they also became an enormous commercial success. Nirvana has sold more than 25 million albums in the United States and in excess of 50 million worldwide. To outside observation, Kurt Cobain had it all. He was married to a beautiful actress/musician who had just borne him a daughter; he had worldwide fame, was a multimillionaire, and had the respect of serious musicians in nearly every genre.

Almost everyone knows the rest of the story, however. At the age of just twenty-seven Kurt Cobain took his own life. He had fought stomach problems for years, was an alcoholic, had been a longtime drug user and had become desperately addicted to heroin. He was also uncomfortable with his success and loss of privacy. Further, he was bipolar and given to bouts of depression.

Attempting to dig through the wreckage of a life like Cobain's is problematic, at best. What part drugs, sickness, and chemical imbalances played in his demise is impossible to say. However, a tiny clue may be gleaned from a note he wrote to his imaginary childhood friend shortly before his death. In it, Cobain expressed that he hadn't "felt the excitement of listening to as well as creating music, along with really writing…for too many years now."

---

[1] Sometimes, you could even understand the lyrics.

MEANING

Somehow, all of Cobain's abilities and accomplishments had lost their meaning to him. In some sense, it had all become pointless.

Meaning Matters

My favorite quote of all time is attributed to the preacher and theologian D. L. Moody: "Our greatest fear should not be that we won't succeed, but rather that we will succeed at something that doesn't matter." This quote resonates deeply with anyone who is anxious not to waste his life. Success is actually no big deal. It's *meaningful* success that's the thing. Now *that's* something. *That's* a legacy.

> "Our greatest fear should not be that we won't succeed, but rather that we will succeed at something that doesn't matter."
> —D. L. Moody

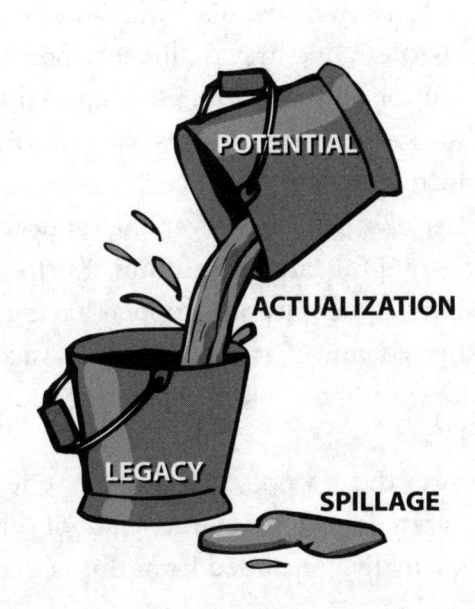

POTENTIAL
ACTUALIZATION
LEGACY
SPILLAGE

Legacy (and Spillage)

You'll remember that in our original diagram of the pails, Legacy is the receptacle into which we pour the time that is given to us. It is the lasting vessel that receives the product of what we do with our lives. It is where what we do is "rescued into the past." Any consideration of legacy must involve an understanding of meaning. Why? Because as Viktor Frankl said, it's "man's deepest yearning." It's an unavoidable pull. It's what our lives are about. We are supposed to matter. We want to matter. We are built to matter. Our legacy should not just be an accumulation of meaningless activities; rather, it should have real meaning.

> **We are built to matter.**

In the introduction to this book, I stated that life is about more than just holding down a job, getting by, or even succeeding financially, finding fame, enjoying ourselves, or accomplishing some mighty task. Ultimately, what we do is supposed to *matter*.

So what, then, does it mean to matter?

In the case of King Pyrrhus, his contributions to the world through violent battles and shrewd alliances produced nothing of lasting contribution to the world. He managed to gain timeless notoriety, but for nothing. Andrew Jackson Brady and my wife's ancestor in the buckboard wagon, conversely, both lived and died in relative obscurity. However, they appear to have contributed to a meaningful family tradition. Kurt Cobain's work entertained millions of people, but stopped having meaning for *him*.[2] He had achieved fame, fortune, and critical acclaim, but his legacy was apparently unbearable because it was empty. Nor is he the only example.

In fact, the list of those who seemed to "have it all" but were insufferably unhappy is as long as the Walk of Stars in Hollywood. What is normally concluded from this is that money and

---

[2] At least, it seems this is a possibility among many others for his tragic end.

MEANING

fame and all the success in the world won't necessarily bring you happiness. While that is true enough, the real truth goes deeper. A better way of looking at it is to realize that nothing in the world brings happiness or lasting satisfaction if it doesn't have meaning. To succeed without meaning is not to succeed at all.

> **To succeed without meaning is not to succeed at all.**

Much of what turns out to have meaning is missed by the world's measurements. The world measures success in terms of money, power, fame, appearance, comfort, and the like. In contrast, what we see in almost any analysis of meaning involves contribution to *others*. It has been quipped that "if we are here to serve others, what are the others here for?" But joking aside, we know deep down inside that we are the happiest when we are serving others. From this, we see that happiness cannot be obtained by direct pursuit. Happiness is the by-product of doing the right things in life. And the "right things" always involve serving and loving and caring and contributing to others. The only way to *be* happy, then, is to *give* happy. The more we give, the more we actually matter, with a side benefit of being happier at the same time. Ultimately, as a Christian, I know that in my life, my utmost fulfillment comes from serving Christ and seeking His glory in all that I do. I don't attempt to do this so that I'll be fulfilled; instead, I notice that I'm fulfilled as a side benefit of doing what I was built to do in the first place—utilizing my gifts and days to glorify and point to my Creator.

> **The only way to *be* happy is to *give* happy.**

This is not to say that we don't want to accomplish something memorable. Nor does it mean that we shouldn't earn money or fame or accomplish mighty achievements. It's just that our accomplishments must bring real meaning into our lives as well in order to fulfill us. And they must be in service to others and to God if they are to really matter.

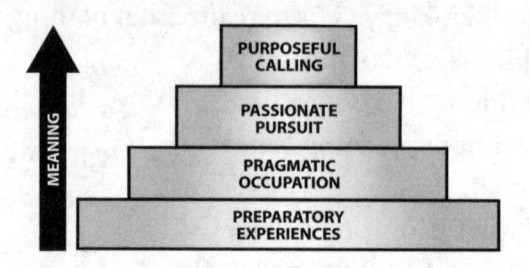

```
         ┌─────────────┐
         │  PURPOSEFUL │
         │    CALLING  │
     ┌───┴─────────────┴───┐
  ↑  │     PASSIONATE      │
  │  │      PURSUIT        │
M │ ┌┴─────────────────────┴┐
E │ │     PRAGMATIC         │
A │ │     OCCUPATION        │
N │┌┴───────────────────────┴┐
I ││     PREPARATORY          │
N ││     EXPERIENCES          │
G │└──────────────────────────┘
```

This brings us all the way back to the ziggurat construct. If our lives are oriented upward toward an overall purposeful calling, supported by fulfilling passions, and undergirded by pragmatic activities, then we will be laser-locked into a life of meaning. It's when there isn't this internal compass that points toward a higher calling that we lose meaning. We may even have strong passions and talents, but if they are not serving a higher purpose outside ourselves, personally, they will be futile.

Going back to Kurt Cobain: Whom was he trying to serve? What was he trying to accomplish? What purpose outside himself was he contributing to with the hours of his life? It's impossible to know, of course, but there are very few traces of anything beyond a few social activisms. These may have been noble, but they don't appear to have been the guiding star orienting his life. One's life drifts aimlessly like a boat with no rudder if it lacks that clear orientation by which to navigate.

Your real legacy begins with what is most meaningful to you personally, and paradoxically, this means it must be external to you and serving a purpose higher than yourself. Without that, you will drift along unfulfilled and empty, succeeding (or not) at something that doesn't really matter. In short:

>It's not as important to succeed
>As it is to matter,

And you'll likely accomplish the former
If you shoot for the latter.

Fall Risk

About a year ago, my mother was in the hospital for hip replacement surgery. In the painful days of recovery, on both the walls of her hospital room and on her wrist were bright orange signs that read, "Fall Risk." This meant, quite obviously, that in her condition, she was a likely candidate for instability and weakness that could potentially cause her to stumble. Always dangerous for senior citizens,[3] a fall for a body that has just received a new hip could be quite terrible. Hence the need for the prominent reminders the signs provided.

In the same way, we humans are unstable and weak and prone to a fall at any time. Of course, I am not referring to a physical fall, as in my mother's case, but rather a moral fall.

It would have been nice to end the chapter earlier. Talking about accomplishment and meaning in one's life can be exciting. But no discussion of leaving a meaningful legacy would be complete without a consideration of the dangers that lurk at every turn which threaten to tarnish or obliterate it. This has nothing to do with success being difficult, as we've already discussed. That discussion revolved around the challenges of climbing the hill. Rather, this is a warning about the dangers of success itself—specifically, the ease with which one can fall from the top of that hill. In the words of the rock group Faster Pussycat, "It's a long way from the bottom and a short drop from the top."

You see, the higher one rises, the more one should be aware of the potential for a fall. The dizzying heights of success also can serve as platforms from which an otherwise well-lived life can plunge to a destructive conclusion. Many a great legacy has been

---
[3] Oh, she isn't going to like that terminology!

ruined by a person's success either "going to his head" or else ushering in unforeseen temptations particular to that lofty position. As we saw in the case of Kurt Cobain, these can be very real.

> The dizzying heights of success also can serve as platforms from which an otherwise well-lived life can plunge to a destructive conclusion.

Stanford University Professor Philip G. Zimbardo said in an interview:

Good people don't rush in to do evil where angels fear to tread; instead, they start by straying only a small way away from their moral center, and each successive step down is hardly different, barely noticeable, until it is too late and their behavior is shocking and may even be…awful.

In the Bible, there are many stories of people who accomplished great and meaningful things, only to fall prey to temptation and sully all they had previously achieved. These "falls" seemed to have occurred in several categories. Noah preached faithfully for a century (without even one known convert) and built a boat to survive the flood but then, after it all, shamed himself with drunkenness. Gideon led the tiny army that defeated the mighty Midianites but then let it go to his head and fashioned gold ornamentation for his own glory. David was called "a man after God's own heart" but then committed adultery and murdered the cuckolded husband. Solomon was called the wisest of all and experienced great wealth and riches but then turned to idolatry. Finally, Judas was a trusted member of Jesus' inner circle but betrayed his leader for money. What do these five examples have in common? These individuals all "fell" from a great height.

We can break down the causes of the five falls given in these examples as follows:

1. Substance Abuse
2. Pride
3. Lust
4. Idolatry
5. Greed

Certainly we could construct a longer list and give even more examples, but I feel confident this list is sufficient to take most of our weaknesses into consideration. When racing through the days of our lives and the pouring of our potential into our legacy, we want to be aware of the snares along the way. None of us is immune to the temptation to fall. None of us lives without dangers lurking in our paths. It is extremely helpful to become aware of the particular sins that have the potential to exert the strongest pull on you and take steps to guard yourself against them. It might even be helpful to envision bright orange signs plastered all over your particular area of temptation proclaiming, "Danger: Fall Risk."

As you pour out the potential of your life into your past, always remember that you are leaving a legacy. For it to have the highest possible meaning, it needs to be free from scandal and shame. Proceed with care because when you look back on your life, you're supposed to be proud of all of it!

– 8 –
Originality

In 1923, a member of the board of directors for Lloyd's Bank in London said to a literary expert at a party: "You may know of one of our employees who is, I understand, a poet: Mr. Eliot."

To which the reply was given: "Indeed, I do. He is a very remarkable poet."

"I am glad to hear it. He is also most proficient in banking. Indeed, I don't mind telling you that, if he goes on in his present way, he will one day be a *senior bank manager*!"

Thankfully for fans of literature the world over, T. S. Eliot didn't settle merely for what he *could* become but instead pressed forward to what he *should* become.

We have discussed the elements of meaning and scandal as they relate to leaving a legacy. These two opposite poles should be ever present in our minds as we live out our lives. We should strive to matter as much as we possibly can and guard ourselves against the inevitable temptations that would cheapen our accomplishments. But leaving a legacy is much more complex and multifaceted than all that. Other elements must be part of the mix. Primary among these is originality.

> There are many things we *can* do, but probably only one that we were *born* to do.

There are many things we *can* do, but probably only one that we were *born* to do.

What Do You Have?

Brad Pitt was a twenty-two-year-old college student at the University of Missouri and just two credits shy of receiving a journalism degree. With only one term paper to complete in order to graduate, Pitt finally admitted to himself that being a journalist wasn't what he really wanted to do.

> I always knew I was going somewhere—going out. I just knew. I just knew. I just knew there were a lot more points of view out there. I wanted to see them. I wanted to hear them. I always liked film as a teaching tool—a way of getting exposed to ideas that had never been presented to me. It just wasn't on the list of career options where I grew up. Then it occurred to me, literally two weeks before graduation: If the opportunity isn't here, I'll go *to* it. So simple. But it had never occurred to me. I'll just go to it.

Just like that, Pitt walked away from college and worked for a couple of weeks at his dad's company to earn some money for gas and travel. Soon after, he was driving west and cheering out loud at every state line he crossed. He had never been as far west as Colorado.

Tom Junod wrote, "Brad Pitt became a movie star before he had been able to make himself an actor. Pitt's secret…was simple enough: He wasn't all that good. But he was already learning how to make his lack of experience and technique his secret weapon." (Director David Fincher said, "Before you are anybody, it's hard to be yourself.") "But," continued Junod, "Pitt had no choice. He had to learn how to be himself in front of the camera, because it wasn't easy for him to turn himself into someone else." And that was Pitt's secret. While most movie fans fawn over actors and actresses because of their talent and ability to portray other characters, moviegoers seemed to like Brad Pitt for himself. Much in the same mold as the likes of John Wayne and Lucille Ball before him (who also had difficulty portraying other characters), Brad Pitt was an original. He was loved for the character that he was, not for the characters that he played.

Sticking with the movie theme, in the film *Walk the Line*, singer-songwriter Johnny Cash's recording studio audition is portrayed as his first big break. The scene begins with his band and him playing a simple, safe gospel song. Sam Phillips, the studio manager, immediately interrupts them. He's not impressed. In what is portrayed as a turning point in Cash's early career, Phillips says:

> If you was hit by a truck, and you were lyin' out in that gutter dying, and you had time to sing one song, huh? One song people would remember before you're dirt. One song that would let God know what you felt about your time here on earth. One song that would sum you up. You're tellin' me that's the song you'd sing?!... Or...would you sing somethin' different? Somethin' real. Somethin' *you* felt. 'Cause I'm tellin' you right now, *that's* the kind of song people wanna hear.

In response to this, Cash and his guys unleash the extremely creative unrehearsed song "Folsom County Prison." It was a piece of music so rare and unusual, so entirely original, that the movie depicts this moment as launching Cash's career. Although the real-life events of Cash's audition at Sun Records weren't nearly so dramatic, and the gospel song the movie rejects was actually recorded by Sun, the point still carries. It was Cash's original work that made his enormous career, not the tried-and-true "safe" recordings others had done over and over previously. Cash became huge in the entertainment world because he was an original. The movie, while taking some dramatic license, certainly expresses that concept correctly.

Mark Twain was a bit of a late bloomer. He drifted around from job to job, headed west to be his brother's secretary in an apparent dodging of the Civil War, worked on riverboats, tried his hand at prospecting for gold, and then gradually became a journalist and finally a writer. He didn't seem to fit any particular mold and became equally popular as a public speaker as well as an author. His novels weren't entirely novels, and his travelogues weren't strictly about travel.

Whatever Twain was, he was certainly an original. In fact, the literary world had never really seen anyone like him before. He seemed not only to break the rules but to laugh at those who followed and enforced them as he did so. This, of course, infuriated critics but simultaneously delighted his audiences. Charles Neider wrote:

> Twain had the artistic temperament without too much of the artistic conscience. His genius was essentially western, its strength the land, the people, their language and their humor. What he lacked was a studied eastern conscience to refine the great ore he mined. Perhaps such a conscience would have inhibited and eventually ruined him. Probably he knew best what was necessary for *him*. What he had, he had in great measure; the naked power of the man with the gift of gab. He knew what a yarn was, and what it was for, and what to do with it… at his best he is uproarious.

ORIGINALITY

In all three of these examples, we see individuals who had shortcomings, lack of experience, and perhaps a narrow band of talent. None of this mattered. They were not held back by what they *didn't* have. Eventually, they were propelled forward by what they *did* have. This is an important lesson. None of us can do much about our gifting and the level of our natural ability. But we can do everything necessary with what we *do* have, with what we *have* been given.

This is not easy, however. It is a big project to discover what is ours and ours alone. In the examples above, none of the three men seemed to have begun with any more than an elusive concept of his innate originality. It took time, courage, perseverance, and work to discover it and tease it out. Again, though, this is where the layer cake or ziggurat concept can help us. Without having everything figured out in advance, we can at least head in the proper direction, knowing that we can figure out the rest as we go. But it is critically important to realize that your greatest contribution will come from your best originality. In the end, your legacy will come from doing what only you can do and in the way that only you can do it. Steven Pressfield wrote, "Our job in this lifetime is not to shape ourselves into some ideal we imagine we ought to be, but to find out who we already are and become it."

> **Your greatest contribution will come from your best originality.**

Your Personal Brand

It happened to you, and it's uniquely yours. No one else has your story. No one else has your particular mixture of experience and ability. Not only did God make you unique in all your parts, but also the life He lets you live is just as uniquely yours. Nobody else experiences the world in exactly the same way as you. These concepts are important to understand because they form the basis of your personal brand.

What is a personal brand?

A personal brand is whatever you do or bring to the world that is entirely and uniquely yours. Perhaps surprisingly, the more you stick to what is uniquely yours and the more authentic you are in what you do, the more interesting it is to others and the more marketable it is.

> **The more authentic you are in what you do, the more interesting it is to others.**

Allow me to give an example.

My wife, Terri Brady, is a very interesting person with a compelling personal brand. Beyond all the foundational things that attracted me to her back in our college days (her love of the Lord, her values and upbringing, her beauty, her courage, her playfulness, her native intelligence, her musical gifts, and above all her undeniable wisdom in choosing me!), she has lived an incredibly interesting and inspiring life. Her list of brand experiences include prolonged infertility, surviving a life-threatening brain tumor, an engineering degree and work experience, homeschooling four children, a consistent record of physical fitness, mastery of multiple musical instruments, dedication to serving in the name of Christ, leading and mentoring many other women, high-level entrepreneurship and business ownership, fabulous public speaking to audiences around the world, and a very popular blog (plus a book based on that blog), not to mention being married to a rascal like me!

In addition to these unique experiences, many of which were beyond her control, the way she carried herself through them is even more impressive. The trials came without complaint, and the victories came without conceit. If you wrap all these things together, you've got one incredible woman with a lot to share.

All these pieces together comprise Terri's personal brand. They make her interesting. They give weight to what she teaches. They give power to what she says.

Now what would happen if Terri tried to teach people about scuba diving or to produce a product focused on fashion? It wouldn't work. It's simply not her. It doesn't fit her brand, and people would sense it subconsciously, rejecting it as false or insincere.

The purpose of this example (beyond a shameless ploy to get points with my wife) is to demonstrate that who we are at the core, in the most authentic version of ourselves, is what we should focus on bringing to the world. When you do precisely that, you will be the most fulfilled. It's when you are doing exactly what you were built to do with the specific gifts God gave you that you feel most alive. Any time you stray away from this reality, you feel less yourself, less alive, less real. Further, though, it is when you strike this authentic chord that the world takes notice. People only want the best you have to offer—nothing less.

> **Who we are at the core, in the most authentic version of ourselves, is what we should focus on bringing to the world.**

The Margaritaville Concept

Jimmy Buffett is an overwhelmingly successful musician and entertainer. He has attracted a following of fanatical fans who dress up in crazy costumes and follow him around on concert tours. He has sold millions and millions of music albums and books. He has a string of successful restaurants and a clothing line. He even has a channel on satellite radio! Over the course of more than four decades, Jimmy Buffett has assembled a massive entertainment empire. And really, when we get right down to it, he did it all with just one song.

If you listen to Buffett's early music, you will notice that it doesn't really match his brand. It's obvious that in those early days, he hadn't really struck the chord of his true, authentic gift, of his personal brand that would someday delight millions. Brent Webster, a musician friend from Buffett's very early days, said about how badly Buffett wanted to break into the music scene: "The impression was, he was trying too hard. His exuberance preceded him."

Twenty-six record companies rejected Buffett. Capitol Records executive Joe Allison said of Buffett in those days, "He pitched some stuff to me, but it wasn't anything I could ever use....His stuff is so off-the-wall, it's hard to think of somebody else doing it. He didn't write like everybody else; he was really different."

As soon as Buffett released the song "Margaritaville" (originally to be titled "Wastin' Away Again in Margaritaville" but changed by Buffett at the last minute), he had found his authentic swing—an escapist genre that whisked people away from their cold, boring lives and put them in the warm tropical sun. According to Steve Eng, "Jimmy's deepening commitment to Caribbean imagery was at once separating him from mere country-rock *and* from new-hippie folkpop. By the mid-seventies, Jimmy was setting, not following, a musical trend."

The song "Margaritaville" won the 1977 BMI pop award, the 1978 country award, and ultimately, the "Three Million Air Award" for that number of radio plays. All this was pretty impressive, but it was only the beginning. The most important part was that Buffett had not only struck upon his true, original gift, but he quickly recognized it. Ever since, with each and every album, song, book, restaurant, and clothing line, Buffett has exploited this very original personal brand.

The image we get here is of an ambitious young musician working hard to make it, searching for his particular and unique personal brand, and then gradually combining all the elements of his life interests into his music. Eng wrote, "Jimmy claims that the Florida Keys theme of his albums wasn't planned; it just evolved naturally." It may have evolved, but once it did, and he discovered this original niche, he built upon it relentlessly.

Imagine going to a Jimmy Buffett concert. You take in the enthusiastic crowd. You sing along with some of the songs. You feel relaxed and happy as you too escape to the islands for a few fun figurative moments. But what would happen if Buffett finished up his concert and failed to play the song "Margaritaville"? You would feel not only disappointed but also cheated. Buffett *has* to perform that song at every concert because it is the classic embodiment of his personal brand, and Buffett, being the consummate entertainer and crowd pleaser, knows this better than anyone.

This principle applies everywhere. How disappointed would people be if Stephen King came out with a marriage book? Or if Dave Barry released a serious novel? Or if Michael Jordan left basketball to play, I don't know, let's say baseball? These people (and every successful person in every walk of life) have succeeded by finding their true, authentic gift and then giving it over and over again with gusto.

> Which brings us back to you.
> What is (or could be) your unique brand?
> What are your particular foundational gifts?
> What are your unique experiences?
> How have you grown, and what can you give as a result of your experiences?
> What innate talents has God given you that are uniquely yours?

What makes you feel the most alive?
What makes you feel the most fulfilled?
What things do you do that seem to bring the most accolades from people?
What could be your "Margaritaville"?

The key is to know yourself, to know *what you have*. You may not be able to answer these questions just yet, and as was true for the entertainers we have considered in this chapter, it might take years for you to discover the answers. But I guarantee that if you answer these questions and package all this together, you will at least be heading in the right direction. Knowing that you should be looking to discover this idea about yourself is a great starting point.

Whether this means you will write books, blog, create music, speak on stages, preach, start a company, paint, organize something, play sports, become a surgeon, lead a charity, invent a new technology, or whatever, if you line things up to be a product of who you are and what you can uniquely contribute, you will succeed. You may not be a musician, but you've got your own, original figurative song to sing. You may not do what you do in the public eye, but you still have a personal brand to discover and build upon. I truly believe that all of us have our own "Margaritaville" waiting to be discovered. By this, I mean that you will find meaning and fulfillment in contributing something that only you can contribute.

Don't live anyone else's life for even a minute. Live yours. It's unique. Find your "Margaritaville," and then sing it with all you've got until you can't sing anymore. Glenn Kelman, CEO of Redfin, said that "what this spun-out, over-hyped world is absolutely famished for is a little genuine personality."

I promise there will be fans cheering for your authentic output. There will always be a market for your original best.

– 9 –
Spillage

If it's true that one way to appear smart is to think of something stupid to say and then not say it, then it should follow that the best way to be efficient is to think of something wasteful to do and not do it.

So far we have been discussing several key elements that comprise our life's legacy. Another set of factors should also be considered, and those are all the things that *don't* make it into our legacy pail but are instead wasted as spillage. For as we pour out the days of our lives from our bucket of potential into our bucket of legacy, we will inevitably splash some out, miss the target, and just contribute less than we were given. There is nothing quite as obvious as wasted potential, but still, the possible scale of such waste can be staggering. Only by acknowledging the ways we waste our potential and spill it into nothingness can we be alert to maximizing our contribution.

Failures

I was in a bookstore one day browsing through the section on historical fiction. I am a sucker for a well-written novel set in a real historical time and involving characters from our past. Thumbing through the familiar names of Bernard Cornwell, Conn Iggulden, and Jeff Shaara, I was surprised to come across a couple of books in this genre by Steven Pressfield. I knew Press-

Legacy (and Spillage)

field to be the creator of the story behind the movie *The Legend of Bagger Vance*, to which I've repeatedly referred. Intrigued, I bought both books and read them with relish. They were remarkable. They transported me back in time, immediately got me interested in their characters, and also taught me much about the epochs in which they were set. Impressed with the breadth of Pressfield's creative ability, I dug into the story of his success.

Apparently, it took seventeen years of trying before Pressfield got his first professional writing job. It was a partnership on a screenplay for a movie called *King Kong Lives*. Excited and confident of success, Pressfield invited everyone he knew to the movie's premiere. Nobody showed. Not a soul. Then the review of the movie in *Vanity Fair* said of Pressfield and the other man who helped write the script, "…Ronald Shusett and Steven Pressfield; we hope these are not their real names, for their parents' sake." Talk about criticism!

Pressfield himself writes of that time in his life:

> Here I was, forty-two years old, divorced, childless, having given up all normal human pursuits to chase the dream of being a writer; now I've finally got my name on a big Hollywood production… and what happens? I'm a loser, a phony; my life is worthless, and so am I.

If the story had ended there for Pressfield, we might never have heard of him. But something happened. In Pressfield's words:

> My friend…snapped me out of it by asking if I was gonna quit…no! [Pressfield answered]. "Then be happy. You're where you wanted to be, aren't you? So you're taking a few blows. That's the price for being in the arena and not on the sidelines. Stop complaining and be grateful."

It's hard to imagine sometimes the resistance and rejection successful people have overcome on their journeys. We look at them and immediately see their genius, their ability, their authentic swing. We know them by their "Margaritaville." But excellence comes only after the long struggle against any and all obstacles that come along. This is easy to forget when looking upon someone who has "made it."

There is another, deeper lesson to be gained from Pressfield's story, however. In effect, he was told not to waste his failure. Specifically, he was reminded to be *grateful* for it!

We have already been through the discussion about how failure isn't fatal as long as it isn't final. But we need to emphasize here that failures are extremely valuable if utilized properly—that is, if they are used as learning experiences and employed in the task of making us better.

Failures hurt. In reading the account of Pressfield's first professional flop, it is easy to feel his pain and embarrassment. But fortunately for thousands of fans all over the world, Steven Pressfield did not allow his humiliations to define him; instead, he let them refine him. The concept is simple but difficult to live out consistently: our failures should not *define* us, but rather they should *refine* us.

> **Our failures should not *define* us, but rather they should *refine* us.**

Too many times, we allow our failures to go to waste. As a result of the pain of failing, we quit, pout, lash out, lose confidence, and lose hope. In such cases, the failures hurt, but they are not allowed to instruct. They knock us down but then are not utilized to lift us higher. They make us appear foolish, but we do not allow them to help us flourish.

Author Frans Johansson wrote:

Groundbreaking innovators...produce a heap of ideas that never amount to anything. We play only about 35 percent of Mozart's, Bach's, or Beethoven's compositions today; we view only a fraction of Picasso's works; and most of Einstein's papers were not referenced by anyone. Many of the world's celebrated writers have also produced horrible books,[1] innovative movie directors have made truly uncreative duds, megasuccessful entrepreneurs have disappointed investors, and pioneering scientists have published papers with no impact whatsoever on their colleagues...the best way to beat the odds is to continually produce.

> "The best way to beat the odds is to continually produce."
> —Frans Johansson

Any life lived will most certainly come with a litany of failures, mistakes, embarrassments, and humiliations. If we are not mature enough to use these shortfalls as stepping stones, they don't find their way into our legacy and are spilled out as waste instead. In such instances, we have felt the pain but not grabbed the gain.

Never waste a failure. Wring from it all the experience and learning you can to come back stronger and better the next time. And no matter what, keep producing.

Time

When it came to emperors, Rome didn't have very many good ones. Although his statue in the Piazza del Campidoglio shows him to have a huge head and buggy eyes, Marcus Aurelius was considered to be one of Rome's better leaders. Also a philoso-

---

[1] I know what you're thinking.

pher, Aurelius famously wrote, "Do not live as though you have a thousand years."

How many clichés are there about the fleetingness of time? How often have we heard not to waste it? Apparently, such admonitions go back at least as far as the Roman Empire. Also, I'm sure we could dig out some Proverbs from the previous millennium, and I wouldn't be surprised if the ancient Egyptians even had something to say about it centuries before that.

Time may be our least replenishable resource. We all know this innately, but our awareness of its passing doesn't seem to have much of an effect on how economically we use it. We let the minutes flow into hours, hours into days, days into weeks, and on and on until we can't believe how much of it has passed and how little we have to show for it.

Have you ever known someone who seems entirely oblivious to the passing of time? They move slowly, have no schedule to keep, and seem to feel no pressure to make use of the sands running relentlessly through the hourglass.

Contrast those people with their opposites: the frenzied, hurried people. Have you known some of them as well? They seem to never be at ease, are always in a hurry, and never have time for anyone else. They are at the constant mercy of a tight schedule. I am reminded of the rabbit in *Alice in Wonderland* who was always "late for a very important date!"

If we are going to accomplish anything worthwhile in life, we need to make good use of our time. This means that we can't behave like those who are oblivious to its passing, but it also means that we shouldn't obsess about it to the point of being frantic. This, indeed, is a difficult balance to strike.

In her book *The Writing Life*, author Annie Dillard made a profound statement: "Who would call a day spent reading a good day? But a life spent reading—that is a good life." I had to think about this sentence quite a bit after reading it. At first, I wasn't

Legacy (and Spillage)

sure I understood what she meant. Then, once I thought I'd gotten it, I couldn't stop thinking about it off and on for weeks afterward. Here is what I took from it: No one can read all day every day; that would be way too taxing and tedious. But the accumulated benefit from a habit of reading at least *some* each day can add up to a lifetime of learning and the enjoyment it brings.

This principle can be extrapolated into a broader application. We can't go to extremes in chasing after every little second of every minute of every hour of every day. That would drive any of us insane and be a terrible way to live. However, we must be ever mindful of the aggregate of time we are given and shepherd it constantly in the right direction. If we spend enough time on enough days doing enough activities consistently in the direction of our highest purposes and calling, the accumulation of this will produce astounding results when lived out over the course of our entire life. This is the key to making the best use of one's time without becoming frenzied and rushed.

Maybe I can make this concept clearer with an illustration from my days of motorcycle racing. At one point in those crazy long-haired teenage years, I was taught that the best racers look the furthest down the track. Amateurs focus right in front of the motorcycle, taking each obstacle one by one in turn, in a first-come-first-served manner. But true professionals look way down the track, not worrying about the next few obstacles but instead keeping their mind fixed on the distant sections of their path.

I tried it for a while and found the results astounding. When I did it correctly, I was much faster. But it was difficult to master, and I continued slipping into the old habit of focusing too closely on just the next obstacle to come along. Eventually though, I learned to look farther and farther down the track, realizing that I could more easily handle all the short-term bumps and ruts if I maintained a longer field of vision.

We all know that we are not supposed to waste our time, but we cannot (and will not) make better use of it by managing every little second and fixating on efficiency. To do so would be like looking no further than the edge of our front fender. Instead, we need to keep a long-term view in mind for what we really, truly want to accomplish overall, trusting that by doing so, we will make the correct maneuvers in the short term.

Dissipation

To achieve the goal of best using our time usually means applying more focus and allowing less distraction. It probably also means saying no to a lot of *good* things along the way so we can more consistently focus on the one or two *great* things.

In some ways, it is odd that Renaissance artist Leonardo da Vinci is so revered today. None of his sculptured works have survived, and a grand total of only about fifteen of his paintings are known. Although he wrote a lot about architecture, no buildings anywhere are credited to his name. Dispassionate scientists have long debated the originality of his many inventions found only in his sketchbooks; little evidence exists that he ever actually built or tested any of these ideas.

Yet Leonardo is heralded as a universal genius, the ideal of the Renaissance in which artists were not only proficient but expected to be masters in many fields. He is shrouded in mystery and myth, with movies and books being written about his sensational secret codes, mischievous messages, and secret handwriting (which was actually just backwards).

As with most postmodern heroes, however, closer inspection reveals a somewhat smaller man. Although it's doubtless he was monumentally talented, Leonardo suffered from what art historian Kenneth Clark called his "constitutional dilatoriness." One of his patrons, Pope Leo X said, "Alas! This man will never do anything!" Leonardo often accepted commissions for works he never finished and, in many cases, never even began. The paintings we know of, such as the *Mona Lisa*, he labored over intermittently for years, and most experts agree that the art itself shows the weaknesses of such a lackadaisical methodology. Perhaps authors D'Epiro and Pinkowish asked it best: "Why did the man who was arguably the greatest painter who ever lived dissipate his energies, often quite carelessly, among so many other fields?"

There is no denying the fact that Leonardo da Vinci was an extremely gifted man, one of the giants of the Renaissance. The question that carries the most meaning for us in regard to our own journeys of life accomplishment is: Why so little output? I am reminded of the Stephen King quote concerning the author of *Gone with the Wind*: "Why didn't she ever write another book?"

Success is the product of many components, of which one of the most prominent is focus. We can do many things in our lives, but we can't do everything. We can have wide interests, and to a certain extent, that is good and healthy, but we shouldn't dissipate our true well of talent on too many endeavors. If genius like that of a Leonardo is wasted by too broad a stroke, then what happens to those of us who are less well endowed? Leonardo himself wrote, "As a kingdom divided against itself cannot stand, so every mind divided among different studies is confused and weakened."

I would posit that the less talented we are, the more focused we must be. Even the least talented can attain grandiose achievements if they apply themselves ferociously, consistently, and with enough focus over time. In fact, it seems that often the greatest ac-

> **The less talented we are, the more focused we must be.**

complishments go to those who actually aren't all that talented but retain just this one last shred of talent: the ability to focus intensely and over the long term.

Sadly, we will never know what wonders of painted masterpieces Leonardo might have produced for the enjoyment of the world. He spent too much of his time elsewhere, on areas other than his strongest gifting. While in many cases, he was still better in these areas than most of the rest of us, the loss still stings. One is left wanting more, but time answers with a heartless "too late." This brings us to the saddest consideration of the squandered gifts of life: What might have been? Leonardo himself wrote toward the end of his life, "*Di mi se mai fu fatta alcuna cosa* [Tell me if anything was ever done]."

Alas, there may not be time for *everything*, but there is time for the *right thing*. With a good amount of focus and a consistent long-term view backed by daily action toward that vision, there will be enough time for what we're supposed to accomplish.

Regrets

"If only I had bought that lakefront property way back when!" "If only I had asked her to marry me before it was too late." "If only I'd tried harder in school." "If only I'd been a little more serious when I was younger." Regrets and "woulda, coulda, shouldas" are part of life for all of us. We have all blown opportunities, missed chances, and somehow squandered important moments. The goal, of course, is to keep these to a minimum while finding a way not to lament overmuch the chances that have gone by. After all, it does no good to keep digging up the past and what we *should* have done. We can learn from our missteps but should never grow demoralized by them.

In the introduction, we considered "The Top Five Regrets of the Dying":

Legacy (and Spillage)

1. I wish I'd had the courage to live a life true to myself, not the life others expected of me.
2. I wish I hadn't worked so hard.
3. I wish I'd had the courage to express my feelings.
4. I wish I had stayed in touch with my friends.
5. I wish I had let myself be happier.

Hopefully the reader will notice that we have been addressing these throughout the book. Overall, the way to avoid these regrets is to use the ziggurat construct to determine the proper direction for your life, stay open to discovering your unique calling and purpose, maintain the course no matter what others may say, and over time, find your true, authentic "Margaritaville" and play it with everything you've got.

As this list suggests, throughout your life, people will try to get you to live the way *they* see fit. Many of them are well meaning and truly care about you, while others, of course, are not. Sometimes, too, it is difficult to tell one group from the other.[2] Ultimately, though, you've got to live your own life. You've got to answer that call you feel deep down inside and do what you were uniquely built to do.

It has been said that one route to unhappiness is trying to please everyone. Instead, we should try to please God first, and we will then find that only in doing so can we be pleased with ourselves.

Further, we only regret hard work when it is meaningless. This is why it is so important to align our lives with what we truly feel passionate about contributing. When we work in line with our passions and in pursuit of the highest calling we detect on our lives (remember your ziggurat diagram and the direction it pro-

---
[2] Especially when it comes to in-laws.

vides for your efforts), we lose the feeling that it is wasted and begin to feel as if it's a privilege. We come to realize that everything we have been given—our resources, our health, our abilities, our time—is part of the raw material we are to use to fashion our legacy. It is then that we realize that our privileges are not for our pleasure but for our purpose.

> **Our privileges are not for our pleasure but for our purpose.**

Know this: Without exception, our purpose will involve others. Our passions, our desires, our ambitions, and ultimately our legacy, will revolve around how well we did serving others with the days and the resources of our lives. This is why it is futile to become task-oriented at the expense of our relationships. Most of our greatest fulfillments in life will come through relationships. They should be given our highest priority. Being a good spouse, parent, grandparent, brother or sister, uncle or aunt, friend, or mentor should be part of any and every focus in our life.

No plan to leave a legacy should slight people or take advantage of them in any way. Quite the opposite: Our life's direction, contribution, and legacy should be with, for, and about people. Forget this one simple truth, and be prepared to suffer the deepest regrets imaginable. Remember it, and you can rest assured that your life will not have been wasted, that not all of your potential was lost in spillage, and that, yes, you did accomplish something because no matter where else you failed, you at least managed to matter to someone.

And that's as important as it gets.

– 10 –
Masterpiece

World War II was the most destructive period of collective human action in recorded history. Tens of millions of people were killed and injured while untold millions more were left homeless and destitute. The destruction of life, property, nations, cities, and cultures was overwhelming, an international tragedy that will forever be a blight on the twentieth century and its philosophies of humanism and humanity's supposed ability to perfect itself.

In the middle of this ongoing catastrophe, caught directly in the crosshairs, was a large proportion of the world's art. These paintings, sculptures, statues, and buildings from throughout the ages were extremely vulnerable to exploding bombs, exposure to the elements, theft, vandalism, and marauding and billeted troops. Masterpieces that in the making had consumed the lives of many of humankind's most talented individuals were powerless against the onslaught of armies crisscrossing Europe.

Nowhere was this more of a concern than in Italy. Home to over one quarter of the world's most revered art, Italy became a white-hot theater of action as the Allied forces worked their way up the peninsula from the south. The German armies dug in ferociously to defend what quickly became the soft underbelly of Europe and their third (and then fourth) open battlefront in the war. Italian citizens, having already surrendered to the Allies by

Legacy (and Spillage)

the time they landed in Salerno, largely turned against their German overlords. Bands of Italian resistance soldiers roamed the land fighting a guerilla war against the Germans. Caught in the chaos and destruction was all that precious, priceless, irreplaceable art.

Impressively, however, all the governments involved took measures to preserve and protect at least some of these artifacts. The US and British troops created Monuments Officers, a cadre of art professors and experts whose job it was to follow the advancing armies and do what they could to rescue or protect art and architecture in perilous positions.[1] They were also involved in bombing briefings to help provide intelligence as to what areas were "safe" to bomb. For their part, the Nazis had a few top-level generals whose actions seemed to indicate their legitimate concern for protecting these treasures as well. Adolf Hitler himself even had thousands of masterpieces stored deep in the confines of Austria's Altaussee salt mines.[2] The Italians, too, were extremely active in attempting to preserve their (and the world's) heritage. Tens of thousands of pieces were first moved into countryside villas for hiding. When the war in Italy evolved from a bombing war into a ground war, however, most of the art was then hurried into the protection of the neutral Vatican in Rome.

According to Robert M. Edsel:

> After evacuating movable works of art, authorities went to work protecting permanent works. Officials wrapped Michelangelo's eight-foot-tall sculpture of *Moses*…in protective cloth, then entombed it in brick. The

---

[1] As this book goes to press, there is a Hollywood movie being made on this very topic!

[2] Of course, many would say the Nazis were involved in systematic theft of these treasures and were only protecting them for themselves. Chief among those accused of such, even by other German officers, was Hermann Göring and his notorious Göring Division.

MASTERPIECE

Arch of Constantine—a triple arch measuring almost seventy feet in height and eighty-four feet in width—was encased using sandbags and scaffolding. Roman authorities even wrapped Trajan's Column in brick.

Similar methods were employed to protect Michelangelo's statue of *David* and many other immovable sculptures in the Uffizi gallery in Florence. Scaffolding, sandbags, and tarps were all that stood between Leonardo da Vinci's *The Last Supper* and total destruction as an Allied bomb obliterated the rest of the Santa Maria delle Grazie Church in Milan. Incredibly, the only wall of the refectory left standing was the one holding up Leonardo's famous painting!

Captain Deane Keller, Monuments Man for the US Fifth Army, said the Italians never questioned his presence or mission. Instead, they cheered. According to Edsel:

> There was always someone knowledgeable and passionate about the town's history and artistic heritage. When [Keller] reached into the back of his jeep and grabbed an OFF-LIMITS sign, a group of townspeople always gathered round nodding and smiling as he nailed it on the wall of a building. Citizens of the liberated cities and towns appreciated his effort.

How is it that people are capable of unmentionably vicious destruction while, at the same time, they can be concerned about the preservation of something as sublime as a work of art? The contrast makes me think of a beautiful flower growing up through the mud and blood of a battlefield. Beauty may be so appealing pre-

> **Beauty may be so appealing precisely because it is so fragile.**

129

cisely because it is so fragile. In its helplessness, it softly reminds us of what Abraham Lincoln called "the better angels of our nature."

Further, we can see that even during a horrendous war, we can still hold in value the greatest masterpieces others have produced. No matter how ugly this world can get, no matter what a mess we make of things, deep down inside, we still know about beauty, and the best of us recognize, cherish, and strive to protect it when we see it.

If we revere the works of human hands to such a degree, then certainly infinitely more valuable must be the life itself that is capable of producing such beauty. Which brings us to the point of this chapter: Our life, and our legacy, must aspire to be a masterpiece. We should approach the living of our life as if it were a great work of art. We should tiptoe up to it gingerly, observe how it appears in varying light, and consider it from all angles before stretching out our hand to advance it toward the fulfillment of what we yet hold only in our imagination.

There are many reasons why this should be so.

Others Are Watching

Barely twenty years after the tragedy of World War II threatened Italy's art, incredibly, much of it was once again in peril. In November 1966, after many days of hard rain, two dams in the Arno river system gave way, discharging over two thousand cubic meters of water each second. Every bit of this tumultuous torrent was headed toward Florence. If Italy houses over a quarter of the world's historic art, then Florence has been said to house easily over half of that.

There was little anyone could do to safeguard Florence's many art treasures, ancient manuscripts, and other artifacts. The floodwaters came too fast and rose too high. In human proportions, the flood was a tragedy, taking many lives. In terms of art, millions of masterpieces were destroyed. No price tag could be placed upon such damage.

Cimabue was a great transitional artist between the Late Gothic and Early Renaissance periods. His fourteen-foot-high frescoed cross, a painting he made in wet plaster affixed to wooden boards in the shape of Christ's cross, was called the "First Page of Italian Art." Painted in AD 1288 and hung high above the altar of the Basilica di Santa Croce, it was moved in 1566 to the church's refectory and hung low on the wall. It remained in this position as the floodwaters of 1966 reached almost twenty feet high.

Ugo Procacci, curator of the Uffizi art gallery and ultimately the man in charge of most of Florence's art, arrived with a small team of assistants shortly after the waters receded. The scene was shocking. Mud several inches deep covered the floor and furniture of the basilica. Worse, the cross of Cimabue was badly damaged by the water. Flakes of paint from the fresco glittered in a million shavings in the mud on the floor. The wood of the cross was saturated and swollen. At that moment, Procacci could take it no longer. In a rare moment of weakness, he broke down and began to cry. One of the attendants there to inspect the damage with him was shocked and said helplessly, "If *you* are crying, what are *we* supposed to do?"

One of the strongest reasons for making your life a masterpiece is because, like the art assistant in the Basilica di Santa Croce that morning, others are watching. And oftentimes, they are watching for how you behave and react in the toughest of moments.

Like it or not, we are all leaders to someone. We simply cannot get through life without becoming an example (good or bad) for others. Sooner or later, and at many points during our lives, we will be

> **Like it or not, we are all leaders to someone.**

called upon to lead. The only question is whether we'll be ready. We already discussed that one of our life's biggest responsibilities is to serve others. This, then, is often how it is done—by setting an example.

Art is a perfect metaphor for how we are supposed to build our lives because art is beheld by gazing upon it. Most art does not involve the other senses (with the exception of music, which can be compared to the words we say). It involves observation. In like manner, so too go our lives. People may listen to what we say, but they put much more stock in what they observe that we actually do.

The Brasini Effect

Let's remain in Italy by considering a fantastic little piece of fiction I read a while ago. In her bestseller *That Summer in Sicily*, author Marlena de Blasi tells the story of a nine-year-old girl sold by her struggling merchant father to a rich prince. The father is coldhearted and cruel and repeatedly spurns the little girl's love and her attempts to return to her familial home.

Once the girl grows up and becomes a woman of her own in the prince's home, she asks him about her situation. The prince assures her he had nothing but the best of intentions for her but asks her a question of his own. He asks her how she managed to emerge from such hurtful abandonment by her father without growing bitter herself. She answered by relating an experience she had had in the village market one morning many years before.

> "I never forgot…The way Signor Brasini just stopped and turned to his wife, put his big farmer's hands out and caressed her face, pulled her close to him and kissed her just like in the films. He kissed her for a long time and then looked at her and smiled.…And when I saw

all that, I knew that their way would be my way. Their way, not my father's...way—their way was how I wanted my life to be. I knew that someday I would be loved by a man like Brasini....*I understood how things worked and how they didn't work.*"

The young girl had found the priceless treasure of a good example. Her whole life up to that point had been cold and full of bitterness. She had been mistreated and neglected. Yet as soon as she saw an example of what *could* be, in fact what *should* be, she was forever transformed. She had seen how things worked and how they didn't have to work.

That's the power of a good example. That's what happens when we focus on making our life into a masterpiece: it allows and inspires *others* to do the same.

One Sentence

George Washington won the Revolutionary War. Abraham Lincoln freed the slaves. Billy Graham preached the gospel. Martin Luther King Jr. fought for civil rights. Roger Staubach played quarterback. Evel Knievel jumped motorcycles. Bill Cosby does family comedy. Pat Sajak hosts game shows. Henry Ford launched the auto industry. Thomas Edison invented the lightbulb. Gandhi peacefully freed India. Nelson Mandela peacefully overcame apartheid. Lech Wałęsa founded Solidarity in Poland. Mother Teresa served the orphans and the dying in Calcutta. Phyllis Diller did comedy. Aretha Franklin is the Queen of Soul. Louis Armstrong brought in the Jazz Age. Lewis and Clark explored the West. Custer got massacred at his "last stand."

This entirely random list of noteworthy people, both dead and contemporary, illustrates a profound insight. Clare Boothe Luce, the first American woman to become a major overseas ambassador[3] for the United States, was also an accomplished author. She once told John F. Kennedy one of the most insightful statements anyone determined to live a meaningful life could hear: "A great man is one sentence."

> "A great man is one sentence."
> —Clare Boothe Luce

What she meant was that the accomplishments, example, or legacy of the greatest people can be summed up in one sentence. Each of the people listed in the paragraph above can have their entire life's work summarized with just one phrase. I didn't come up with those sentences myself. I played a little game with many different people and told them to respond with one sentence to describe each of the people on the list. What resulted was a strikingly similar list of answers. In some cases, you may note, the answers aren't even exactly accurate. Nonetheless, that is how history has come to categorize what each person did, stood for, contributed, or accomplished.

When it comes to leaving a legacy, it might do you wonders to think through this idea of a single sentence to summarize *your* life. If you died today, what do you think that sentence would be? What would you *like* it to be? Are they one and the same? Or is it too soon to tell? Perhaps you've got a single sentence you'd *like* to have said about you and your life's contribution. If so, does that align with your current path and actions? If not, what changes do you need to make to get things heading in that direction?

By the way, as we said earlier, nearly everyone desires to have a sentence such as "was a good mother," "was a good dad," "was a good husband," etc. These are monumentally (excuse the pun) important. But having a sentence beyond that, something bigger, something more, is not a bad thing. Accomplishing something else significant does not have to come at the expense of being a

---

[3] To Italy and then Brazil.

wonderful family member. I say this because many people come up with nothing more than familial summarizations, and this is fine, as long as it doesn't become an excuse to go no further with one's life. For who's to say what you were built to do except for you and your Creator? It's up to you to discover and determine, and it might just surprise you!

Back to Gandalf

This book was written to answer the puzzle posed by Gandalf in the movie *The Lord of the Rings: The Fellowship of the Ring*. Do you remember what it was? "All we have to decide is what to do with the time that is given to us." By this point, I hope that you've developed at least a basic understanding of how to go about making such an important decision and, further, how to actually live it out.

Socrates once said, "The unexamined life is not worth living." Guy Kawasaki then took it one step further, writing: "The unexamined life may not be worth living, but the unlived life is not worth examining."

My friend Tony Tefel once sent me a creative text, a parody on a nursery prayer we've all heard. It is simple but stunning. I have kept it stored in my phone for just this moment. It went like this:

> Now I lay me down to sleep,
> I pray the Lord my soul to keep,
> If I should die before I live,
> I pray the Lord my sin forgive.

In essence, the way to answer Gandalf's question is by posing another:

Twenty years from now, what will you wish you had done today?

If you fulfill that wish on a regular basis, you will be on your way to assembling your life as a monument.

Make it a masterpiece.

EPILOGUE

This book was intentionally and painstakingly kept short. At many points during its construction, I was hard-pressed to stop myself from fleshing out the concepts further. This, tempting as it may have been, would have violated the spirit of the book as an approachable, brief, and hopefully enjoyable guide to living a life that counts.

In no category was this struggle for brevity more pronounced than in the massive topic of seeking God's will. After all, how could I write a book about fulfilling potential and leaving a legacy without answering the question plaguing so many Christians, namely: What would God have you do?

First, I did not leave out the consideration of God's will. Several times, I attempted to make the point that your decisions should be based upon prayer and faithfulness to God's calling on your life and through His gifting in it. The whole point of the ziggurat construct was to point you upwards toward your highest calling. Ultimately, this comes from God.

Second, what I also did not do was allow the flow of thought to bog down in the widely varying theological interpretations among different Christian camps as to just what it means to seek and act upon God's will.

The biggest part of God's will for us is unmistakably clear in the pages of Scripture. As Mark Twain famously quipped, "It's not the parts of the Bible I don't understand that bother me!" God wants us to be saved, filled with the Spirit, sanctified (holy), submissive to His authority, and to suffer if necessary for His sake. This is not my list; it's from author John MacArthur's wonderful little book *Found: God's Will*. I would highly[1] recommend that any sincere Christian read this book. Another fabulous little work on the subject is *Just Do Something* by Kevin DeYoung. Putting these two simple but powerful books together will bring much clarity and peace regarding finding and following God's will in your life. They will also (I hope) fit perfectly into what I've written in these pages. In fact, this book and its instructions were intended to pick up where those two books leave off. What I mean by this is once a Christian has figured out the big picture of God's will for his life, how does he figure out the details in between? It is my sincerest hope that this book has provided a useful answer.

---

[1] And I mean highly.

ACKNOWLEDGMENTS

Every book is a team effort, no matter whose name appears on the cover. My wife and bestselling author Terri Brady deserves recognition for not only allowing me the mini-sabbaticals necessary to research and write this book, but for the heroic role she plays in sharing an adventurous life. Thanks also to my children Casey, Nathaniel, Christine, and J.R. for their patience and attention at many a dinner-table lecture, and especially to Casey and Nathaniel for allowing me to use their soccer playing as an example in chapter 4.

Thank you also to my parents Jim and Gayle Brady, and particularly my mom for providing the illustration of her professional career in chapter 1. Thank you to my friend Dr. Doug Bookman for the quote that appears in chapter 6 and to my friend Tony Tefel for the poem that made for such a great ending to the book.

A special thank you goes to Orrin and Laurie Woodward. Your belief that this book would be both good and important drove me forward.

A talented cast of characters prop me up professionally. Special thanks go to my lifelong friend and COO at Life, Rob Hallstrand. Thanks also to "Chip the Kip" Karnish for his many great ideas and promotional efforts. As always, Bill Rousseau deserves my gratitude for keeping me on schedule while managing a million of my projects at the same time. And Deborah Brady (no relation) deserves hearty thanks for editing the manuscript and making me appear literate. Thanks also to Wendy Branson, who has to absorb all my nit-picking emails with class, and to Ryan

Renz and his media staff, who, being real artists, always make me feel like I am one, too. Norm Williams, whom I've worked with now for almost 15 years, continues to do a world-class job with graphic design and deserves thanks for designing the cover. Thank you also to Steve Kendall for wrapping his arms around the entire book-making process and truly putting Obstaclés Press on the path to greatness. Thanks also to Oliver DeMille for a very helpful early reading of the manuscript. I also wish to thank my personal assistant Doug Huber, who smoothes out my life on a daily basis, and Tracey Avereyn for keeping my social network rocking.

I also wish to thank my great friends and business partners George and Jill Guzzardo, Dan and Lisa Hawkins, Holger and Lindsey Spiewak, Wayne and Raylene MacNamara, Felmar and Sandra Montenegro, and Curtis and Debbie Spolar. Your partnership is as cherished as it is enjoyable.

And finally but primarily, I wish to honor my Lord and Savior Jesus Christ. May my life be a ziggurat that points to Him.

OTHER BOOKS BY CHRIS BRADY

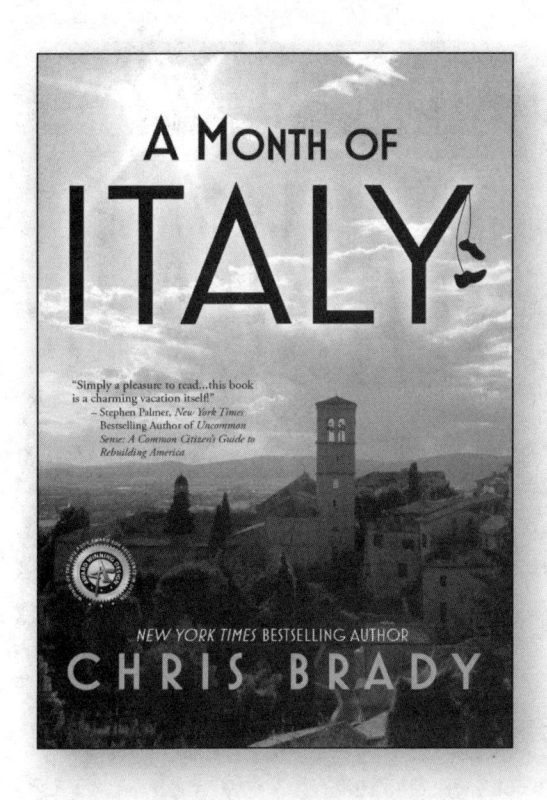

A MONTH OF ITALY

"Simply a pleasure to read...this book is a charming vacation itself!"
~ Stephen Palmer, *New York Times* Bestselling Author of *Uncommon Sense: A Common Citizen's Guide to Rebuilding America*

NEW YORK TIMES BESTSELLING AUTHOR
CHRIS BRADY

Winner of a
2013 Gold ADDY Award

Featured in
the Major Motion Picture
A Long Way Off

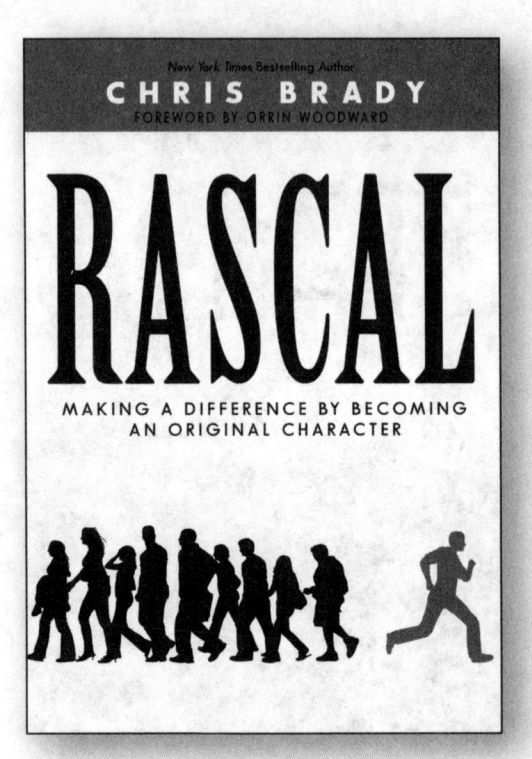

**GOLD MEDAL
WINNER OF THE
2013 LIVING NOW
EVERGREEN
BOOK AWARDS**

CHRIS BRADY

Chris Brady is a *New York Times* best-selling author, speaker, humorist, and businessman. His books include *Launching a Leadership Revolution* (co-authored with Orrin Woodward), *PAiLS*, *Rascal*, *A Month of Italy*, and several other titles on leadership and success. He has sold nearly 2 million books in 9 languages. Chris is the CEO and Creative Director of The Life Platform. He is also the executive publisher of Obstacles Press, and one of the Founders of All Grace Outreach, a 501(c)(3) charitable organization. Chris is listed on the *Inc. Magazine* Top 50 Leadership and Management Experts and is one of the Top 100 Authors to Follow on X/Twitter. In 2017, he was listed *Richtopia's* Top 200 list of most influential authors in the world. Chris serves on the following non-profit boards: Italy for Christ, Wisdom International, All Grace Outreach, and Triangle Literacy Council. Chris and his wife Terri have four adult children and two grandchildren and live in North Carolina.